# ZEAMI, BASHŌ, YEATS, POUND

# STUDIES IN GENERAL
# AND COMPARATIVE
# LITERATURE

*Volume I*

1965

MOUTON & CO.

LONDON · THE HAGUE · PARIS

# ZEAMI, BASHŌ, YEATS, POUND

## A STUDY IN JAPANESE AND ENGLISH POETICS

*by*

726

MAKOTO UEDA

1965

MOUTON & CO.

LONDON · THE HAGUE · PARIS

LIBRARY OF CONGRESS CATALOG CARD NUMBER: 65-28168

*Printed in The Netherlands by Mouton & Co., Printers, The Hague.*

# PREFACE

There have been a number of studies on the nature of poetry, but most of them treat the subject within a single cultural tradition. This book is an experimental attempt to go beyond this practice and bring together the ideas of poetry conceived by the people of different traditions. Such a method will involve some serious disadvantages: it tends to underestimate, among other things, the historical continuity of literature and structural difference between unrelated languages. Yet the method, when properly applied, will have at least one justification: it will help to illuminate some essential features of poetry which transcend the difference of language and literary convention.

The four writers of the title have been chosen because they seem to have certain factors in common. All of them were practising artists rather than systematic theorists, yet as they happened to live in the times of transition they had to create and develop their own ideas on the nature of art and poetry. Furthermore, these four writers are related to one another by what is usually termed as literary influence. Yeats wrote several plays which he called the *nō*. Pound, one of the earliest translators of the *nō*, also helped to introduce the *haiku* to the West. The question of influence, however, will not be dealt with at any length here, except in places where it directly throws light on the nature of poetic art.

The main methodological difficulty lies in the fact that these writers wrote about poetry from widely different angles, using their own literary terms and idioms. If the chaotic state of literary criticism in our time is considerably due to the lack of agreement in critical approach as well as in aesthetic nomenclature, that is all the more true in the case of our four writers whose times and places range from the 15th-century Japan to the 20th-century United States. Zeami, in particular, may seem to stand distinctly apart from the other three because he was primarily concerned with the art of acting rather than with the technique of poetry. Yet his problems were ultimately not dissimilar from those of the other three: he, too, was deeply involved in such questions as life versus art, the nature of beauty, or the relation between art and religion. For Zeami there was little difference between art and poetry, between aesthetics and poetics.

In a like manner, efforts will be made to seek a common ground where the four writers may meet on the same terms. Zeami and Bashō, specifically, are almost entirely unknown to the West except through their imaginative works; consequently the vocabulary they used in their critical essays will have to be explained. In the process of such explanation the terms and ideas of Western poetics will be employed, but one should never forget that they are, after all, arbitrary. Questions as to whether the *nō* is classical or romantic, or whether the *haiku* can be called a lyric, will not enter our discussion because our present concern is with those ideas which are more elementary than Western scholars' distinctions and categorizations. Along this line, the first four chapters of the book will expound each writer's ideas on poetry in general conceptual terms, interpreting and clarifying his literary idioms while discarding all the ideas which interested his circle, his time or his cultural tradition alone. The final chapter will, by comparing and synthesizing the four writers' attitudes, attempt to illuminate some universal essentials of poetry not affected by the difference of language or literary convention.

This book was originally prepared as a doctoral thesis at the University of Washington in Seattle. I owe sincere thanks to Professors Frank W. Jones, Richard N. McKinnon and Charles Gulluns for reading the manuscript in its initial stages of preparation and offering a number of invaluable suggestions. I am especially grateful to Professor Jones for his genial guidance in the general conception and method of this work, and to Professor McKinnon for his expert advice on Zeami, Bashō and numerous other topics in Japanese literature. However, I alone am responsible for all the errors and inadequacies this book may contain.

The first two chapters of the book have appeared in the *Journal of Aesthetics and Art Criticism* in a somewhat condensed version, and I should like to thank its editors for permitting me to use the same materials again. My acknowledgements and gratitude are also due to the following editors and publishers who generously gave me permission to quote from the writings of Yeats and Pound: to Mrs. W. B. Yeats and the Macmillan Company (London and New York), for permission to quote from W. B. Yeats, *Essays* (1924), *Collected Poems* (1957) and *Autobiography* (1953); to Chapman & Hall, Ltd., for permission to quote from the *Collected Works of William Butler Yeats* (1908); to Mr. Allan Wade and Rupert Hart-Davis, Ltd., for permission to quote from the *Letters of W. B. Yeats* (1955); to Alfred A. Knopf, Inc., for permission to quote from Ezra Pound, *Pavannes and Divisions* (1918); to New Directions, for permission to quote from Ezra Pound, *The Spirit of Romance* (1952) and *Polite Essays* (n.d.); to Mr. D. D. Paige and Harcourt, Brace & World, Inc., for permission to quote from the *Letters of Ezra Pound* (1950); and to Yale University Press, for permission to quote from Ezra Pound, *Make It New* (1935).

M. U.

# CONTENTS

# CHAPTER I

# ZEAMI MOTOKIYO: IMITATION, *YŪGEN*, AND THE SUBLIME

A certain Japanese poet, commenting on the difference between the artisan and the artist, once said that the latter always strives to explore and expand the meaning of his art
while the former simply tries to fulfil the rules handed down
by the tradition. Zeami Motokiyo[1] was known to his contem-
poraries largely as a master artisan, yet we now know him as
a rare artist. Born as the eldest son of a great *nō* performer, he
followed his father's footsteps and came to achieve great fame
for his acting, chanting and dancing; his contemporary
audience enjoyed his art, quite possibly without knowing
what lay behind it. Yet, although we now cannot in any way
restore Zeami's performance, we do have a way to learn some
of the ideas he conceived on the art of the *nō*. These are expressed in a body of his miscellaneous essays, written at various
times of his career, aiming, primarily, to make practical advice
on the training of actors, principles of acting, play-writing,
dancing and music, and numerous other matters relating to
the performance of the *nō*. Despite the variety of topics with
which the essays deal, one cannot fail to recognize Zeami's
never-failing passion for the perfection of his art: "a man's life

[1] Zeami Motokiyo (1363-1443), actor, playwright and theorist, is
assumed to be the author of the majority of the plays in the present *nō*
repertoire. His essays on the art of the *nō* were not made public until 1909.
Important among them are *Fūshi kaden* (*The Flower of the Form*, 1400-02?),
*Shikadō* (*The Way to the Highest Flower*, 1420?), *Nōsaku-sho* (*The Book on the
Writing of the Nō*, 1423?), *Hana no kagami* (*The Mirror of the Flower*, 1424?),
*Kui* (*The Nine Ranks*, 1427?), *Sarugaku dangi* (*Discourse on the Nō Drama*,
1430?), and *Zeshi shichijū igo kuden* (*Teachings of Zeami after Seventy Years
of Age*, 1433?).

has an end", he says, "but there is no end in the pursuit of the *nō*".[2] In fact his essays were written in order to set a high goal toward which the best of *nō* performers in the succeeding years were expected to strive. On the other hand Zeami was not an idealistic theorizer who merely played with abstract ideas. The essays reveal him to be an efficient, realistic, and at times even shrewd person: his scheme of actor-training is devised with the details which remind us of a curriculum at some modern professional school; he was so practical even as to warn that an actor should take a look before his performance to make sure that no nail was sticking out on the stage.

The first basic principle in Zeami's concept of art is that of imitation. "Objects to be imitated are too many to be enumerated here", he says. "Yet they have to be thoroughly studied since imitation is a foremost principle in our art." Then he adds: "The basic rule is to imitate things as they are, whatever they may be."[3] A *nō* performer should carefully observe the speech and deportment of princes, ministers of state, courtiers and warriors; he should ask them, when he meets them after his performance, whether his acting has been an acceptable imitation of what they actually say and do. When he is cast in the role of a high court lady he can rarely see, he should inquire of the traditional manner in which such a lady speaks and behaves, or of the customary ways in which she wears her clothes. The imitation of an ordinary woman is easier, as one can observe a model anywhere and at any time. Some *nō* actors, too intent on producing the effect of elegant beauty which they thought was the aim of the *nō*, often neglected the principle of imitation. Zeami warns sharply against such negligence. It was not that he thought lightly of artistic effect; on the contrary, he considered the principle of imitation as fundamental in creating an appropriate aesthetic

[2]  *Hana no kagami*, in Asaji Nose, *Zeami jūrokubu-shū hyōshaku* (*Zeami's Sixteen Treatises: Texts and Commentaries*. Abbreviated as *ZJH* hereafter), I, 423.
[3]  *Fūshi kaden*, *ZJH*, I, 35.

sentiment. In a passage where he speaks of forcefulness and elegance as two important qualities of the *nō*, he says:

In any act of imitation, if there is a false element, the act will become coarse or weak ... For instance, it will be a false imitation to create the forceful out of the weak; the act then will become coarse. To act forcefully for the things forceful – this is forceful, and not coarse. If an actor departs from the principle of imitation in the hope of producing elegance out of something forceful, his act will not look elegant but weak. Therefore, if an actor gives himself up to this principle and becomes at one with the object of his imitation, his performance will look neither coarse nor weak. Also, when a forceful thing is imitated more forcibly than it should be, the performance will appear especially coarse. If one tries to be more elegant than what is appropriate to the occasion, one's performance will look especially weak ... Such unfortunate cases occur when the actor assumes that there is such a thing as elegance or forcefulness apart from the things they imitate. These two exist in the forms of things themselves. Court ladies high and low, men and women beautiful and refined, various kinds of flowers – these are the things whose forms are elegant in themselves. Warriors, rustics, devils, deities, pine trees – these may be thought of as forceful things. When accurately imitated, the imitation of an elegant thing will become elegant, and that of a forceful thing forceful ... Forcefulness or elegance does not exist by itself. It springs from an accurate imitation of an object. Weakness or coarseness arises when the actor fails to observe the principle of imitation.[4]

Art imitates nature in order to reproduce what nature has. Any act of imitation which distorts nature for the sake of an artistic effect will result in either coarseness or weakness; it is artifice, and not art. An aesthetic effect like forcefulness or elegance is inherent in the natural objects themselves. The actor, therefore, should try to bring himself into the heart of the natural objects rather than to bring them into the subjective sphere of his mind. He should minimize the activities of his ego; a personal element should not enter the process through which an object in nature is transformed into its equivalent in art.

Zeami further develops his idea of non-personal quality in artistic imitation and comes to reject the actor's conscious

[4] *Ibid.*, 190-197.

will toward imitation. "In the art of imitation there is a stage called 'non-imitation'", he says. "If one proceeds to the ultimate of imitation and entirely enters the thing he is imitating, he will possess no will for imitation."[5] In the highest stage of imitation the actor becomes unconscious of his art; the imitator is united with the imitated. And he can do this only when he completely projects himself into the essence of the object which he imitates; the man and the object become at one in the essence they share with each other. Zeami calls this essence the "true intent". A *nō* performer, in a more elementary aspect of imitation, will try to represent the things of life as they are. But, over and above this, he should endeavor to express the "true intent" of the thing; for the sake of the "true intent" he might not make an exact copy of the outward appearance. In point of fact it is impossible to imitate realistically a demon from hell, the ghost of a butterfly or the spirit of a pine tree; the object of imitation is often supernatural in the *nō* drama. Still, such a thing could be convincingly represented if the artist successfully creates the feeling of its "true intent". "Nobody has seen a real demon from hell", says Zeami. "It is more important, therefore, to act the role in such a manner as to deeply move the audience, rather than to attempt to imitate the demon."[6]

What Zeami exactly means by the "true intent" is difficult to define, but we may have a fair idea of it as we read his comment on the art of acting a frenzied man's role. He writes:

It is extremely difficult to play the roles of those who are mentally deranged because of various obsessions, such as a person would experience at the parting with his parent, at the loss of his child, or at the death of his wife. Even a fairly good actor does not distinguish between different obsessions but portrays frenzied men all in a similar manner; the audience, therefore, is not impressed. A man is frenzied because of an obsession; therefore, if the actor makes the obsession the true intent of his portraiture, and the frenzy an effective expression of it, then his acting will certainly impress the audience and create a breathtaking climax. If there

[5]   *Ibid.*, 227.
[6]   *Sarugaku dangi, ZJH*, II, 351.

is an actor who moves the audience to tears by such means, he is a performer of rare greatness.[7]

The "true intent" of a character, then, is the inmost nature that constitutes the core of his person. In a frenzied man mental derangement is merely the outward expression of an inner cause; the deepest truth in this person lies in his obsession, or what has caused the obsession, rather than in his madness. One who wants to portray such a man will try to represent that specific obsession, instead of merely copying the features of any madman; he will imitate the characteristics of a frenzied man in such a way that the primary cause of the man's madness may manifest itself. Realistic details do not much matter; or rather, it would be better if they are eliminated wherever necessary for the sake of the "true intent". A good actor, Zeami implies, should pierce through the surface of everyday reality and reach for the hidden truth of things. Only then the effectiveness, or beauty, of a performance will be attained.[8] Zeami's idea of beauty is thus closely related to his interpretation of life. *Yūgen*, his ideal beauty, is not only an aesthetic principle but a mode of perception. The term, originally used in Taoism and Buddhism, literally means something mysterious and profound which lies beyond the reach of ordinary human senses. Since it was imported from China and employed in literary criticism in Japan, *yūgen* had been greatly expanded in meaning and came to imply a kind of beauty which is elegant, remote and subtle. Yet its original meaning, with its mystical overtone, always stuck to the term. "*Yūgen* is ultimately a sentiment inexpressible in word, a landscape unseen in form", says a thirteenth-century scholar. "As its sentiment has profound truth, and its word utmost beauty, the effect naturally springs from it."[9] Zeami, inheriting the tradition, advocates *yūgen* as the final goal for the

---

[7]   *Fūshi kaden*, *ZJH*, I, 48.
[8]   Cf. Yoshie Okazaki, "Nō no hongi setsu" (On the True Intent of the *nō*), *Geijutsuron no tankyū*, 73-93.
[9]   Kamo no Chōmei, "Mumyōshō" (Nameless Selections), *Nihon kagaku taikei*, III, 312.

art of the *nō*. After explaining the manifestations of *yūgen* in various character types, he goes on:

An actor should master all these character types so that he can successfully cast himself into any of them at will. But, whatever kind of imitation he performs, he should never depart from the principle of *yūgen*. This will be like seeing a noble princess, a court lady, a man, a woman, a monk, a peasant, a humble man, a beggar, an outcast, all standing in a line each with a spray of blossoms. Although they differ in social status and outward appearance, they are equally beautiful blossoms insofar as we feel the effect of their beauty. The beautiful blossoms are the beauty of human form. The beauty of form is built by the creative spirit.[10]

*Yūgen* is not a superficial surface beauty; it lies deep in the heart of things. Therefore, even an imitation of something which is not externally beautiful may be made beautiful if the inner beauty finds its way out. A withered old man, ugly in appearance, can be made to have certain beauty: Zeami describes the beauty as "blossoms blooming on a dead tree". A dreadful demon of hell can be made beautiful too: Zeami describes it as "blossoms blooming on a crag". What creates real beauty is the "creative spirit". Zeami uses the term in many different ways, but basically it seems to imply a spirit in pursuit of the highest type of beauty. To learn the "spirit" of composition, one should carefully study classical poetry; to learn the "spirit" of mimicry, one would better start with the imitation of elegant people. An actor should firmly get hold of what makes a person or thing beautiful, and attempt to embody this essence of beauty in his performance. Zeami aptly explains this process of artistic transformation with an anatomical metaphor – the bone, the flesh and the skin.[11] The bone is the spirit that tries to discover and express ideal beauty; it is "pre-art", as it were, and this sometimes enables a genius to attain an amazing success even at a very early stage of his training. The flesh is that part of art which can be learned by training. The skin corresponds to artistic effect; it is the visi-

---

10    *Hana no kagami, ZJH*, I, 362.
11    *Shikadō, ZJH*, I, 459-467.

ble part of art. A human body consists of the bone, the flesh and the skin, although we see the skin only. Similarly, the beauty of the *nō* consists of personal inspiration, traditional framework and external action, although the audience sees only the last of the three. Zeami emphasizes the harmony of these three elements as essential to a successful performance.

Yūgen, then, is inner beauty of things outwardly expressed by means of art. It is the manifestation of the "true intent" which lies in the depth of things. In this sense it is identical with truth – the truth caught by the artist's "creative spirit". The mysterious feeling which *yūgen* connotes comes from its pursuit of hidden truth. Outward reality is illusory; there is higher reality lying somewhere beyond the reach of our ordinary senses. The artist, seeking for ideal beauty, instantaneously penetrates the surface reality and gets a momentary hold of hidden truth. Such a romantic concept of reality would lead anyone to prefer the elegant past to the degenerate present, the refined few to the uneducated mass. Whether this was the primary motive or not, Zeami particularly yearns for the lost world of the Heian period wherein artistic taste was most highly cultivated. Characters in *The Tale of Genji* such as Lady Aoi, Lady Yūgao and Lady Ukifune, are the most precious heroines of the *nō*. In the golden years of the Heian period men and women in the court, with their most refined taste in art, lived always in search of ideal beauty; delicate, subtle, elegant beauty was their very life, the force that kept their lives going. A *nō* actor, therefore, may imitate the appearance and manners of a court lady in minute detail, while he should not do so when he acts a woodcutter's role. A court lady, knowing what refined beauty is, has made herself look so; a woodcutter, who does not know it, needs the actor's art to be made beautiful. The imitation of a court lady, as Zeami teaches, is the basis of all the other imitations. When this kind of beauty is elevated to its highest level, it will give the impression of "a white bird with a flower in its beak".[12] The

---

[12]    *Ibid.*, 478.

famous metaphor suggests Zeami's romantic aspiration after the purest type of beauty, after a creation of unearthly beauty by means of art.

Yet it is in the very essence of *yūgen* that this elegant beauty is combined with a feeling of sadness. If *yūgen* is a mode of perception into the hidden nature of things, it cannot but bring out a pessimistic notion of life. For the law of the universe prescribes that even the most beautiful lady must suffer the hardship of life, that even the loveliest blossom must fade away. Immediately after stressing the importance of elegant beauty in *nō* performance, Zeami says: "But there are even more precious materials for producing the visual effect of *yūgen* than the elegant appearance of court ladies I have just referred to; these rare examples are seen in such cases as Lady Aoi haunted by Lady Rokujō's spirit, Lady Yūgao carried away by a ghost, or Lady Ukifune possessed by a supernatural being."[13] *Yūgen*, then, lies not simply in the graceful beauty of a court lady but in such a lady going through an intense suffering – a suffering caused by a power beyond her control, by the law of causation, by the supernatural, by the unknown force of the universe. Such a suffering naturally leads to sad resignation. The court lady, lacking the masculine courage to heroically fight with her fate, surrenders to religion when she comes to realize that suffering is the condition of being alive in this world. *Yūgen*, in the final analysis, may be conceived as a combined quality of elegant beauty and sad resignation – the elegant beauty which is a result of man's quest for his ideal through art and artifice, and the sad resignation which comes from man's recognition of his insignificance before the great cosmic power that rules over this world. Thus Zeami defines *yūgen* as "elegance, calm, profundity, mixed with the feeling of mutability".[14]

Of these two elements of *yūgen* Zeami stressed the first much more than the second in the earlier part of his career; in those

[13]  *Nōsaku-sho, ZJH,* I, 614.
[14]  *Ongyoku goi,* in Kazuma Kawase, *Tōchū Zeami nijūsanbu-shū* (*Zeami's Twenty-Three Treatises, with Notes*), 83

years *yūgen* was almost equivalent to graceful beauty. Yet as he grew old the emphasis was reversed: he came to admire cold, subdued beauty more and more. Already in one of his early essays there is a suggestion of this when he confesses his preference of a withering flower to a fully blooming one. Later he becomes more explicit: he says that a superb actor, when he acts an important scene, will "perform chanting, dancing and mimicry in such a manner that the audience may, without knowing it, be deeply impressed by the subdued simplicity of the atmosphere".[15] Elsewhere Zeami calls this kind of acting a "chilled performance" and ranks it the highest of all performances.

In this respect it is interesting to observe how Zeami categorizes *nō* plays in some of his later essays. He classifies the *nō* into five types by the over-all effect which each play exerts upon the audience. He seldom tries to define the effect in analytical terms; instead, he cites a poem and a plant which are supposed to produce a similar emotional impact; he also illustrates his point by quoting passages from actual *nō* plays. These five types are called "celebration", "*yūgen*", "longing", "grief", and "the sublime".

The drama of "celebration" is a little different from other types in that a happy mood pervades it. A play which belongs to this category celebrates the order of the universe ruled by heaven. "Its mood", writes Zeami, "is peaceful and devoid of any malignant thought".[16] The play sings out the happy voice of the people who live in a well-governed nation. Its effect may be compared to that of a pine tree with its evergreen needles, or to a classical Japanese poem:

> May our august Emperor
> Live for thousands of years
> Like a venerable pine tree,
> So that we may all live
> Peacefully under his shade![17]

---

[15]  *Hana no kagami, ZJH,* I, 396.
[16]  *Ongyoku goi, Tōchū Zeami nijūsanbu-shū,* 82.
[17]  *Goongyoku jōjō, ZJH,* II, 152.

This type of *nō* drama presumes an optimistic view of life. There is order in the universe ruled by heaven; there is order in the nation ruled by the Emperor; man, in this world, wants to live as long as he can. The audience will feel joy and happiness as he sees this type of play acted.

The second type of drama is based on the first type; only there is an added element – graceful beauty. If the drama of "celebration" is a piece of undyed fabrics, that of "*yūgen*" is a piece of textile deeply dyed by sentiments, as if "white threads were dyed in five colors".[18] Its beauty is what we would feel as we "look over the morning scene of spring flowers and the evening scene of the autumn moon". Its impact is like that of cherry-blossoms:

> Snowy petals scatter
> At the cherry-blossom hunting
> On the field of Katano:
> Shall I ever see again
> Such a beautiful spring dawn?[19]

The image of cherry-blossoms falling like snow neatly combines the purity of beautiful whiteness and the sense of life's mutability, adequately introducing the sentiment of the last two lines. Although here *yūgen* has dwindled into a quality which characterizes one of the five types of *nō* drama, Zeami never forgets to emphasize its importance: he adds in a parenthesis that "*yūgen* is an element common to all five types". He also states that it will not be necessary to quote many examples "because all the *nō* plays and folk dances since the Ōei years [1394-1427] are of *yūgen* type".[20]

The third type, called "longing", is defined as the "further deepening of *yūgen*".[21] If the effect of *yūgen* is something like the cherry-blossoms falling in spring, that of "longing" is like maple leaves turning in autumn. The sentiment is more specific and personal than *yūgen*; it is particularly associated with

18   *Ongyoku goi, Tōchū Zeami nijūsanbu-shū*, 82.
19   *Goongyoku jōjō, ZJH*, II, 152.
20   *Ibid.*, 158.
21   *Ongyoku goi, Tōchū Zeami nijūsanbu-shū*, 83.

love between men and women. Love is beautiful, but does not last long in this transient life; it is always followed by sorrow. The feeling embodied in this type of *nō* can be illustrated by this poem:

> In the autumn wood
> Where the lower leaves of maples
> All start to fall,
> A deer, wet in the evening drizzle,
> Lonesomely calls for its mate.[22]

If there is in *yūgen* something which implies a sentiment of sad resignation, it has become a more immediate feeling here – it is the sorrow of a husband over his lost wife. On the cosmic level the "longing" is a longing for permanence in nature. On the personal level it is a longing for eternity in love. In neither case can man expect his wish to be fulfilled, whereupon sorrow ensues.

The fourth type, "grief", goes still one step further. It is a sentiment that will lead one to "grieve and shed tears". It is a sentiment one would feel over his friend's death. "Spring blossoms and autumn leaves are all fallen", Zeami explains. "Objects in sight are the wind blowing over the high mountain peaks, the tops of thick-growing trees, and the desolate wilderness covered with zebra grass."[23] If spring and autumn represent the sentiments embodied in *yūgen* and "longing" respectively, winter is the season for the fourth type of plays. The sentiment may be illustrated by this poem:

> Even on a mountain
> Insensitive to injury
> There grows the *nageki*, or
> The Bush of Sorrow. What wonder
> If it grows in this deserted heart![24]

The sentiment is quite personal: it is the grief of a woman deserted by her lover. In the second and third types the poets vaguely hinted their melancholy moods in a cluster of nature

---

[22] *Goongyoku jōjō, ZJH,* II, 152.
[23] *Ongyoku goi, Tōchū Zeami nijūsanbu-shū,* 84.
[24] *Goongyoku jōjō, ZJH,* II, 153.

images; here in the fourth type the poetess directly utters her acute pain in words. The straightforward statement of personal suffering replaces the vague suggestion of universal sadness.

The fifth type, "the sublime", is the one which Zeami ranks the highest among all styles. One can reach this realm only after he has mastered all the other four types. The performer will unite "the orthodox and the unorthodox in one sound, and sing in a usual yet unique tone".[25] There is the liberty of a man who has thoroughly learned the restricting rules of art and finally transcended them all. There is neither spring, autumn, nor winter: there is only the dignity of a cedar tree which grows green throughout the four seasons:

> Slowly, quietly,
> The spear-shaped cedar tree
> On Mount Kagu
> Came to have an air of austerity,
> With its root under the moss.[26]

This is somewhat different beauty from *yūgen*. Instead of the gay, colorful loveliness of cherry blossoms, it has the silent, quiet dignity of an old cedar tree. If *yūgen* is the graceful, flowering beauty of youth, "the sublime" is the calm, subdued beauty of old age.

Zeami further clarifies his idea of "the sublime" as he grades the different styles of the *nō* drama into nine ranks. One who wishes to learn the art of the *nō* should start with the sixth rank and work upwards from there. When the student finishes the fourth-ranked style and enters the third, his performance will begin to assume the air of "the sublime".[27] This style, the lowest of the highest three ranks, is called the Style of a Calm Flower. Zeami explains:

The Style of a Calm Flower:

> "Snow is heaped in a silver bowl."

When snow is heaped in a silver bowl, the sight is pure in white

---

[25]  *Ibid.*, 140.
[26]  *Ibid.*, 153.
[27]  Cf. *ZJH*, I, 553-554.

glimmer, with a true feeling of softness somewhere in it. This may be called the Style of a Calm Flower.[28]

The actor shows the ease of an artist who is confident of his art after mastering all the required stages of craftsmanship; his performance, as a consequence, is not obtrusive but "calm", not rigid but "soft". A silver bowl, a wonder of art, contains snow, a wonder of nature, and both the container and the contained are united in the purity of whiteness.

A style one step higher than the Style of a Calm Flower and which ranks the second among the nine styles is called the Style of an Infinitely Deep Flower. Zeami says:

The Style of an Infinitely Deep Flower:
> "Snow has covered thousands of mountains all in white.
> Why is it that one solitary peak remains unwhitened?"

A man of old once remarked: "Snow does not disappear from Mount Fuji because it is so high." A Chinese disagreed and said: "Snow does not disappear from Mount Fuji because it is so deep." What is exceedingly high is deep. Height has a limit. Depth is not to be measured. Therefore, the mysterious scene of one peak not being white among thousands of snow-covered mountains may represent the Style of an Infinitely Deep Flower.[29]

Elsewhere in the same essay Zeami comments: "The Style of an Infinitely Deep Flower is the ultimate form of *yūgen*. It is a style which reveals the middle ground where being and non-being meet". A performer who has the Style of a Calm Flower is still in the world of being, the world of ordinary reality, even though his art may have the purest beauty of snow in a silver bowl. An actor who has advanced to the Style of an Infinitely Deep Flower goes beyond the limitations of empirical reality; an irrational element, like a black peak towering among snow-covered mountains, may come into the world which his performance creates. His art is beyond our measure; it is like a deep sea whose bottom lies somewhere in the mysterious unknown. The actor may do something which would be in conflict with our common sense, but we are so overpowered

[28]  *Kui, ZJH*, I, 547.
[29]  *Ibid.*, 547.

by his performance that we forget the irrationality of something being black when it is usually white.

Yet still this style is surpassed by another, a style which ranks highest of all. This supreme style, the perfection of art, is called the Style of a Mysterious Flower. Zeami remarks:

The Style of a Mysterious Flower:

"In Silla the sun shines brightly at midnight."

The "mysterious" means something which cannot be explained in words, something which cannot be thought in human mind. It is like the sun shining at midnight, a phenomenon which transcends the expository capacity of speech. The profound art of a rare master in the *nō* cannot be adequately described by any word of praise. It leads the audience to a state of trance; it is a styleless style which surpasses any scheme of grading. A style which yields such an impression upon the audience may be called the Style of a Mysterious Flower.[30]

A little later Zeami adds that this style conveys "an imaginative landscape which is beyond verbal description as it lies in the realm of the absolute". The realm of the absolute, a term taken from Zen Buddhism, implies a sphere where there is neither good nor evil, neither right nor wrong, neither one nor all. The sun shining at midnight, which is a flat contradiction in ordinary reality, is perfectly acceptable in this realm. Silla, the present Korea, is located to the east of China; the sun is already rising there when it is still night in China. What seems to be a flat contradiction to our ordinary senses may be a profound truth when it is viewed from a point which transcends the limitations of time and space. Above our everyday reality there is a higher reality which ordinary human faculties cannot sense. When we face a good work of art we are unwittingly led into such a realm, where we are made to perceive the invisible and hear the inaudible.

Thus the *nō* drama may be considered as an art which attempts to illuminate internal and external reality reflected in the deepest depth of the mind's eye, a level of reality which cannot be known through ordinary senses. The world of the

[30]  *Ibid.*, 547.

*nō* is primarily that of the subconscious. Two things which would be contradictory to one another in the realm of the conscious are made to co-exist in the *nō* drama, like the sun shining at midnight. It is a remote, shadowy and eerie world where primeval emotions aimlessly flow, a world which has little to do with ethical codes or social conventions. In contrast to the realm of the conscious which is complex and superficial, the world of the *nō* is simple and profound as it is liberated from the controling power of the ego. It has no place for laughter, because wit and humor are manifestations of intellect. It does not admit the individuality of each man, since it presumes the identity of all men beneath their conscious minds – the "collective unconscious", as one of our contemporary scholars has pointed out.[31] No person who appears in the *nō* is given real characterization.

We may then understand the *nō* drama as a ritual to bring this "other world" into our own living sphere. The monk, who is the deuteragonist in many a *nō* play, is the priest for the ritual, the medium who conjures up a dead man's soul from the underworld. The soul who is called up naturally takes over the protagonist's role in the *nō*. He narrates the story of his life – his soul-life which covers the yonder world as well as the present world, and his story constitutes the core of the play. The audience is expected to believe that the protagonist makes his appearance in the monk's dream; the dream provides a means to bring the two worlds together.

The implications of the *nō* drama are necessarily religious rather than ethical, because any issue of human life which it deals with is seen not in terms of human society but in relation to the cosmic law that governs man both in life and in death. Man may be able to control the conscious part of his mind, but the subconscious is beyond his power, it belongs to the all-inclusive universe. Zeami seems to have recognized some great primal force which flows through life and death, through the conscious and the subconscious; it manifests itself in the

[31] Cf. Yoshitaka Takahashi, "Nō no bigakuteki kōsatsu" (An Aesthetic Study of the *nō*), *Bungaku*, XXV (1957), 1028-35.

"true intent" of every object in nature. He says that "one contains many while two are just two", referring, perhaps, to the same concept.[32] An artist should try to represent this invisible energy of the cosmos by means of symbolism. Zeami, in one of his most suggestive passages on art, remarks:

If I may illustrate my purport by the principle of two ways in Buddhism, being and non-being, then the appearance will correspond to being and the vessel to non-being. To take an example, a crystal, although it is a pure, transparent object without color or pattern, produces fire and water. Why is it that two entirely heterogeneous things like fire and water emerge out of one transparent object? A poem says:

> Smash a cherry-tree,
> And you will find no blossom
> In the splinters.
> It is in the sky of spring
> That cherry-blossoms bloom.

The seed for the flower of art is the artist's soul which has a power to feel. As a crystal produces fire and water or a colorless cherry tree bears blossoms and fruit, so does a superb artist create a variety of works out of his imaginative scenery. Such a man may be called a vessel. Works of art, treating the wind and the moon or flowers and birds, accompanying a festival or a picnic, are many and various. The universe creates thousands of things as the seasons roll on – blossoms and leaves, the snow and the moon, mountains and seas, trees and grass, the animate and the inanimate. The artist should try to attain the Mysterious Flower by letting these numerous things be the materials of his art, by making his soul the vessel of the universe, and by setting the vessel in the vast, windless way of emptiness.[33]

Zeami recognizes the existence of two worlds, the world of being and that of non-being. The one is the world we can perceive through our senses, the world of appearance. The other cannot be easily seen because it is hidden beneath the surface; it can be felt only by the sensitive soul of an artist who has a power to feel. The artist creates his work out of his own

[32]   *Fūkyoku-shū*, *ZJH*, II, 121.
[33]   *Yūgaku shūdō fūken*, *ZJH*, I, 536.

soul, just as the universe creates thousands of things out of itself; the artist, as well as the universe, is a vessel which contains potential creative energy. The artist's soul is expressed through the things of the universe; here the human and the cosmic, the microcosm and the macrocosm, become at one.

This is, we may say, an animistic mode of perception. In natural science there is a clear distinction between the subjective and the objective, the mind which sees and the object which is seen. An observer with a scientific mind, in his effort to grasp an object outside of himself, carefully examines the object and minutely analyzes it. Such a method will ultimately lead to naturalistic realism in the field of literature. Zeami's idea stands exactly at the opposite pole. His ideal is the union of the subjective and the objective, the observer and the observed, in the sphere of the scientifically impossible. The union is made possible only when one recognizes some super-human soul latent in all the things of the universe. An artist ought to catch this invisible spirit and present it through the things visible.[34]

This being the ultimate aim of art, the artist must rely on symbolization rather than description in attaining it. A symbol may lead one to an instantaneous perception of what cannot be analyzed or described. Man, for instance, often feels an irrational yet irresistible desire for something that is beyond his power. Instead of a Dr. Faustus or an Iago, the *nō* writer creates a butterfly of late spring aspiring to the plumblossoms of early spring (*Kochō*). A more complex symbol, to take another instance, is a plant called a sacred tree. On the cosmic level it represents permanence in nature, since it is an evergreen tree. On the human level it symbolizes constancy in love, since in a famous episode of *The Tale of Genji* a branch of a sacred tree is given by a man to a woman as a token of his unchanging love. On the religious level the name explains itself: the sacred tree signifies eternal God who rules both man and the cosmos. All these different levels of meanings are

[34]    Cf. Yoshishige Abe, "Nōgaku to kokuminsei" (The *nō* and National Traits), *Nōgaku zassō*, 65-81.

combined, in an imaginative way, within the image of a sacred tree and appeal to the reader in an instant of time. Furthermore, the sacred tree is made not only a poetic symbol which is conveyed to us through the reading of the text or listening to the chant, but also a dramatic symbol that can be actually seen on the stage. The protagonist appears on the stage with a branch of a sacred tree in her hand (*No-no-Miya*).

The *nō* writer's method of grasping reality by intuition rather than by reason, and his way of presenting it through symbols rather than through statements, link the *nō* closely to the fine arts. Some people have noticed the resemblance of the *nō* to painting and sculpture. Everyone knows that the *nō* drama actually contains dancing and music. The relation of an ordinary drama to painting and sculpture is not a particularly close one, because the drama, restricted by time and movement, tries to make the most of its dialogue and action; consequently the beauty of an ordinary drama is that of one continuous whole, not of one movement or of one moment which is a part of the whole. But the *nō*, because of its emphasis on intuition, minimizes the elements of time and movement; one little movement in a lengthy duration of time is made to suggest a great deal. In other words the *nō* drama, primarily a time art, is made to approach the realm of space arts. Thus a certain painter says: "The *nō* can be said to be a drama richest in elements of painting ... At times it has a tempo so slow that it almost appears to be a succession of several *tableaux vivants*. Each of the actor's movements constitutes an excellent composition of painting, its elegant form of straight lines never being disturbed by the movements."[35] A certain sculptor remarks:

The *nō* has the elements of sculpture more than any other histrionic art. I even feel as if the *nō* were an extension of sculpture ... The *nō* studies how one can move with the minimum of movement ... Every movement in the *nō* is pure, definitive, final. Therefore, even the slightest movement has forcefulness. It is like the water-

[35] Ikuma Arishima, "Nō no kaiga bi" (Pictorial Beauty of the *nō*), *Nōgaku zensho*, VI, 79.

less substance of human movement, while a movement in our daily lives is always diluted with water.[36]

The pictorial and sculptural elements of the *nō* are crystalized in the *nō* masks. If sculpture and painting (particularly Japanese *sumi* painting) ultimately attempt to represent the essence of human emotion, the *nō* masks aim at that too. While the actor's own face is always a personal expression of a universal sentiment, a *nō* mask embodies the impersonal expression of a personal emotion.

Dancing is a very important element in the *nō*. Zeami says:

One should know the way in which singing and dancing in the *nō* are derived from a single spirit. When the spirit remains in the mind, it is called emotion; uttered in words, it is called poetry. When one cannot stop with poetry alone, he goes on to sing it out, waving his hands and stamping his feet in ecstasy.[37]

The passage draws heavily on the Major Preface of *The Book of Songs*, a well-known Chinese classic, and it shows the commonly accepted notion of poetry and dancing in Zeami's time. Poetry is an expression of a personal emotion, and when the emotion becomes more intense it takes the form of dancing. Dancing, in its origin, is a spontaneous expression of emotion, a subconscious act, in contrast to our daily behavior which is in the main the result of our conscious thinking and will. It is significant that a dance in the *nō* drama is always performed by the protagonist – that is, a ghost, a deity, a mentally deranged person. What the protagonist wishes to express reaches the level beyond the conscious; it cannot be stated in logical terms; consequently there is need for symbolism in writing it out, for dancing in acting it out. As the language of poetry is highly stylized and evocative, so the movement of dancing is highly restrained and suggestive. Every action of the dancer has a symbolic meaning, because it is always an expression of some inner feeling. A *nō* play reaches its climax with a dance, as dancing signifies the most intense form of man's

[36] Kōtarō Takamura, "Nō no chōkoku bi" (Sculptural Beauty of the *nō*), *Nōgaku zensho*, VI, 83-85.
[37] *Ongyoku goi*, *Tōchū Zeami nijūsanbu-shū*, 81.

psychical energy. It may even be said that a *nō* play is built around its climactic dance.

Music is an even more significant element of the *nō* drama. "Chanting is the soul of the *nō*", Zeami says. "It is most essential for the *nō* actor to master this art."[38] Acting and dancing emerge out of chanting, and not *vice versa*. For one thing, a *nō* play itself has a musical structure. Teaching how to compose a *nō* play, Zeami says:

> The writing of the *nō* consists of three stages. The first stage is to get the material of the *nō*. The second is to compose the music. The third is to write the text. The writer should first of all study his material carefully. He should then construct the three portions of the musical structure – introduction, development, climax – in such a way that they are well fitted into the five scenes of the play. Finally he should collect proper words and write the text in accordance with the musical structure.[39]

Music plays an essential role in the making of the *nō*; it is a primary principle by which the material of art is transformed into a work of art. The *nō* text is written always in accordance with a musical structure. This implies that each *nō* play has a musical structure. As a rule a *nō* play consists of five scenes, and from the standpoint of music the opening scene constitutes the introduction, the three middle scenes the development, and the last scene the climax. Introduction, development and climax are musical terms originally used in China, and would in a very rough way be compared to the three parts of a sonata movement – exposition, development and recapitulation. The introductory part is dominated by a slow, regular-beat rhythm, which appears most clearly in the passage where the itinerant monk sings of his travel. The development part breaks this regular rhythm with the appearance of the protagonist who sings in a different tone and tempo, converses with the monk and then goes on to narrate the story of his life. The climax is characterized by a quick, irregular rhythm as the protagonist, revealing his true identity, re-enacts the scene of his crime and

[38]  *Sarugaku dangi, ZJH,* II, 385.
[39]  *Nōsaku-sho, ZJH,* I, 590.

the resulting torments of hell. This, of course, is a general rule and a variation is quite permissible. Yet, whatever liberty the *nō* writer may take will not break away from the principle of structural coherence through music.

The principle of musical unity within a play is extended to a whole performance which, if orthodox, consists of five plays. The first play is generally a play of "celebration" where the order of the cosmos and of the nation is praised; it has the regular-beat tempo of an orderly life and the slow-moving rhythm of a ritual thanking deities for the peaceful world. The second, third and fourth plays constitute the development: they are usually apparitional plays, and their rhythms range from a fairy's exquisite music to a mad mother's dance of frenzy. The fifth play, called the "hobgoblin play", has in its climax an irregular, quick-moving rhythm which accompanies a dreadful demon dance. The musical quality in the *nō* thus gives unity to the different parts of a single play on the one hand, and to a sequence of different plays on the other.

Zeami repeatedly emphasizes the importance of a union between music and drama in the *nō* performance. He says, for example, that one of the secrets of success in the *nō* performance is the "Opening of the Audience's Ears":

The "Opening of the Audience's Ears" refers to a certain part of a *nō* play where two sets of the audience's ears are united in one impact. It is in this part that the ultimate meaning of the play is written out and the ears of the audience's mind are opened, that, at the same time, the words which embody the meaning fit the music which accompanies the words. When the meaning and the music are felt to be united in chanting, everyone in the audience will be deeply moved. Such a manifestation of meaning and music in one unified feeling is called the "Opening of the Audience's Ears".[40]

Meaning and music are, as Zeami states elsewhere, originally two different things; they are understood and enjoyed through two different sets of ears. Yet when a performance reaches its climactic part the two become one: music becomes expressive

[40]  *Ibid.*, 643.

of meaning and meaning comes to enhance the beauty of
music; philosophical implications and sensory effects are perfectly united. Music is the most sensuous of all arts; the *nō*
writer, who attempts to say something that cannot be said
through analytical reason, naturally depends on music in the
most important part of his work. He tries to appeal not to
intellect alone or to emotion alone, but to the whole body of
the person who watches his performance. The combination
of poetry, music and dancing greatly increases the dimension
of the impact which the drama exerts upon the audience.

   Thus the language of the *nō* drama must be melodious and
picturesque. Zeami compares it to the flowing water in a
stream: the chanter's voice is the water, and the chanting is
the stream. The stream goes through its different phases, now
slowly flowing on the plain, now violently rushing in the
rapids. The *nō* writer should "create a garden with all kinds
of water-scenes – with a winding stream, with lofty rocks, with
beautiful falls".[41] Chanting ought to be highly evocative,
with numerous visual and auditory images. The language of the
*nō* must be melodious: "Phrases should be linked together in
such a way that the whole sounds smooth, pleasant, and softly
flowing."[42] The *nō* text is highly poetic. In fact Zeami, who
advises *nō* writers to give up all the other pursuits in order to
devote themselves entirely to their profession, makes an
exception for classical Japanese poetry. The *nō* writer should
carefully study the works of good poets, because "the secret
of *nō* writing lies in the linking of various words and phrases
used in classical poetry".[43] The diction of classical Japanese
poetry is very refined, colorful and melodious, yet compact
because of its short thirty-one syllable form. Density of texture
is another of Zeami's principles of composition. "Know the
fragrance of words", he says. "The basic principle of composition is to convey meaning in the briefest words."[44]

[41]   *Fushizuke-sho, ZJH,* II, 89-90.
[42]   *Ongyoku kowadashi kuden, ZJH,* II, 8.
[43]   *Fushizuke-sho, ZJH,* II, 86.
[44]   *Sarugaku dangi, ZJH,* II, 478.

The *nō* drama, then, is primarily poetry rather than drama; it is poetry acted on the stage. It imitates human actions, but it does so in such a way as to reveal the hidden essence of man and things, the "true intent" which only the sensitivity of the artist can feel. Naturally the *nō* writer is concerned not so much with social or ethical problems as with the issues of man's deepest self which lies beyond the realm of the conscious. He approaches the issues not through a reasoned analysis or a metaphysical system, but through an instantaneous perception, an emotional understanding, which is possible as he submerges himself in the things that surround him. He sees life through death, being through non-being, permanence through change. *Yūgen*, Zeami's ideal beauty, can be understood to be such a mode of perception; it is not merely inherent in the things observed but lies in the way the observer looks at things. The fact that Zeami's notion of beauty is intrinsically related to his attitude toward life is also evident in his classification of *nō* plays: celebration, *yūgen*, longing, grief, and "the sublime". *Yūgen* and "the sublime" are primarily the words to describe aesthetic effects, while celebration, longing and grief imply optimistic or pessimistic views of life. The highest type of drama, "the sublime", presents an illusion of life as seen from a perspective which transcends life; there is the feeling of calm resignation as the author recognizes a cosmic power that rules man as well as animals and plants. In order to convey such subjective, imaginative truth, the playwright not only makes a profuse use of images and symbols, but incorporates music and dancing into his drama. The language of the *nō*, consequently, is also highly musical and symbolic.

To Zeami the *nō* must have meant something just as serious as religion. In fact the basic ideas which underlie his notion of art are close to those of Japanese Buddhism. It was art that gave him a way to come in contact with invisible reality; it was the way to attain true happiness. We certainly admire Zeami for his most sincere devotion to art rather than sneer at him for his superstition when he tells us that one night in 1412

a Shinto deity appeared in his dream and asked him to perform ten *nō* plays for dedication.[45] Yet we also feel that he
was after all one of our fellow men when he tells us he too had
some moments of doubt, grief and suffering. A passage which
he wrote at the age of seventy seems to imply his realization
that art is not religion after all; he wonders whether his strong
attachment to art does not constitute a drawback from the
attainment of Nirvana.[46] Zeami's ideas on art, embodied in
his essays, deserve our high admiration because they reveal
him to be a great artist and artisan. Yet at the same time they
make an immediate appeal to our hearts as the record of a
man who suffered the conditions of human life as we all do,
who turned to art looking for a way toward salvation, and
who, with all his devotion, still remained short of an enlightened state.

[45]   *Ibid.*, 583-584.
[46]   *Zeshi shichijū igo kuden, ZJH,* II, 667.

# CHAPTER II

# MATSUO BASHŌ: THE POETIC SPIRIT, *SABI*, AND LIGHTNESS

Matsuo Bashō,[1] the poet who perfected the *haiku* as a serious
art form, shows a marked resemblance to Zeami in some respects. In a sense he was a medieval poet living in a modern
age. He declared his adherence to medieval Japanese poets
such as Saigyō and Sōgi, and, like them, he followed the footsteps of Li Po and Tu Fu in his way of life. He was also much
attracted to Buddhism, particularly to Zen Buddhism.
Medieval Buddhism tried to save men from life's tortures by
the motto: "Meditate on death". Although he never entered
the priesthood, Bashō was often a hermit who found meaning
in life through contemplation of death. There were, however,
some unmistakable traits of modernity in Bashō, too. His
*haiku*, unlike *waka*[2] or the *nō*, was distinctly an art for common
people. It required neither an elaborate costume, classical
scholarship, nor courtly elegance of style. Bashō's *haiku* is
characterized, among other things, by colloquialism and
humor. It does not describe heaven and hell; it finds its

---

[1] Matsuo Bashō (1644-94) was born in a samurai family, but left home
as a youth and spent most of his life traveling through various regions of
Japan and composing *haiku* poems along the way. His ideas on the nature
of poetry are suggested in his prose works such as "Genjū-an no ki" (The
Unreal Dwelling, 1690), "Heikan no setsu" (On Closing the Gate, 1692),
"Saimon no ji" (The Rustic Gate, 1693) and "Oi no kobumi" (A
Traveler's Scribble, 1709), as well as in his letters to his pupils. But it is
in the writings of the two leading disciples under him, Kyorai and Dohō
(see notes 3 and 5), that Bashō's poetics fully reveals itself.
[2] A form of classical Japanese poetry. Also called the *tanka*. It consists
of five lines, with 5, 7, 5, 7 and 7 syllables each. Since around the ninth
century it had been an art almost exclusively for the upper class.

materials in everyday life. It does not grieve over the mutability of life; it gazes at man's mortality with smiling eyes. In Bashō, to "meditate on death" does not necessarily deny the pleasures of life. He sees life and death from a distance, from a place which transcends both.

Bashō wrote no systematic treatise on the art of *haiku*. Whereas Zeami tried to prevent future deterioration of his art by leaving its secrets only to the best-qualified of his followers, Bashō traveled far and wide, and extended his teaching to anyone interested in *haiku*. It seems he taught different things to different persons; at times, two of his teachings are so different that the one almost seems to contradict the other. Perhaps Bashō wanted to cultivate his pupils' talents rather than to impose his own theory upon them. Or, perhaps, he did not approve of any fixed doctrine in *haiku*. The latter point was meditated on by Bashō himself, who developed it into the idea of "permanence and change" in art.

Bashō's comments on "permanence and change" were made on various occasions, and apparently not always with exactly the same implication. Yet his central idea is sufficiently clear in the following remark, recorded by Dohō:[3]

In the Master's art there is that which remains unchanged for thousands of years; there is also that which shows a temporary change. Every one of his works is ascribable to the one or the other, and these two qualities are the same in essence. This common essence is a true "poetic spirit". One does not really understand the *haiku* unless he knows the permanent style. The permanent style is the one which is firmly based on the true poetic spirit, irrespective of the writer's time or of the contemporary fashion ... On the other hand, it is a principle of nature that things change in numerous ways. In *haiku*, too, nothing new will be born unless it transforms itself with time.[4]

An artist always aims at the universal, yet tries not to lose his

[3] Hattori Dohō (1657-1730), one of Bashō's leading disciples. His *Sanzōshi* (*Three Books on the Art of Haiku*. Completed not long after Bashō's death, but not published until 1776) is one of the most reliable records of Bashō's teachings on the *haiku*.

[4] *Sanzōshi*, in *Shōmon haiwabun-shū* (abbreviated as *SH* hereafter), 162.

identity. Bashō, facing the dilemma, attempts to find a solution in a dialectic. He approves of both styles, permanent and
temporary; a "permanent" poem is good because it embodies
an eternal truth, and a "fashionable" poem also is interesting
because it has freshness. Yet, as Bashō sees it, they are really
the same in essence. Everything changes in our life; change is
the only permanent thing. We observe seasonal changes, but
they are equally the manifestations of the force in nature:
flowers, leaves, winds, clouds, snow – they are created by a
single spirit in nature. Similarly, there is a "poetic spirit"
which lies in all great works of art. This spirit is timeless;
only the ways in which it is expressed may change as time
goes on. One of Bashō's disciples, Kyorai,[5] loosely interprets
this as a dualism of "substance" and "manner". The interpretation is valid only in a limited sense: "substance" must
mean certain ingredients which give a timeless quality to the
poem, while "manner" should imply an individual way in
which this quality is expressed.

The next question, and a very important one, is exactly what
Bashō means by the term, a "poetic spirit". His answer seems
to be suggested in one of his most famous passages:

There is one common element which permeates Saigyō's *waka*,
Sōgi's linked verse, Sesshū's painting, and Rikyū's tea ceremony.
It is a poetic spirit, through which man follows the creative energy
of nature and makes communion with the things of the four seasons. For those who understand the spirit, everything they see
becomes a lovely flower, and everything they imagine becomes a
beautiful moon. Those who do not see the flower are no different
from barbarians; those who do not imagine the flower are no
different from beasts. Detach yourself from barbarians and beasts;
follow the creative energy and return to nature.[6]

---

[5] Mukai Kyorai (1651-1704), one of the best poets among Bashō's
followers. His *Kyorai shō* (*Selected Writings of Kyorai*. Published 1775),
containing many informal conversations between Bashō and himself, is an
excellent material to learn Bashō's ideas on the *haiku*. The passage in
question appears in "Kyorai no monnan ni kotauru no ben", *SH*, 423-424.
Kyorai wrote another book on the principles of *haiku*, called *Tabine-ron*
(*Sleeping on a Journey*, published in 1778).
[6] *Oi no kobumi, Bashō ichidai-shū* (abbreviated as *BI* hereafter), 572.

In other words, Bashō believes that there are two types of men, those who possess a poetic spirit, and those who do not. While the latter type of people are blind to natural beauty, the former seek it in every possible way and thereby try to eccape from the collisions of everyday life. Saigyō, Sōgi, Sesshū and Rikyū were engaged in different branches of art; but what made them great was the same – the recognition of beauty in the creation of the universe. The recognition, moreover, was of a particular kind: it was spontaneous, intuitive perception which was possible only when the spectator identified himself with a natural object, or with the energy flowing in the object. Hence comes the notion of "return to nature".

This concept naturally leads Bashō to the idea that an artist should insert no expression of his individual ego into his work. Dohō has recorded:

The Master once said: "Learn about pines from pines, and about bamboos from bamboos." What he meant was that the poet must detach himself from his will. Some people, however, interpret the word "learn" in their own ways and never really "learn". "Learn" means to submerge oneself within an object, to perceive its delicate life and feel its feeling, out of which a poem forms itself. A poem may clearly delineate an object; but, unless it embodies a feeling which has naturally emerged out of the object, the poem will not attain a true poetic feeling, since it presents the object and the poet as two separate things. Such is a work of artifice made by the poet's will. [7]

Beauty in nature is a manifestation of a supreme creative force which flows through all things in the universe, animate and inanimate. This force, it must be stressed, is different from the creative power of an individual physical being. The energy of the universe is impersonal; it produces the sun and the moon, the sky and the clouds, the trees and the grass. The energy of individual man is personal; it roots in his conscious will, in his passions and desires, in his egotism. But man, being part of the universe, also has impersonal energy within him, an energy which he shares with the cosmos. It is this energy

---

[7]    *Sanszōshi, SH,* 162-163.

which every poet must work with in his creative activity. Bashō, therefore, does not share the view that a poet puts his own emotion into a natural object and gives airy nothing a local habitation and a name. On the contrary, he believes that a poet should annihilate his personal emotion or will for the sake of impersonal energy within him, through which he may return to the creative force that flows in all objects in nature. One may attain this ideal state through a devoted contemplation of a natural object. One should try to enter the inner life of the object, whereupon he will see its "delicate life" and touch its "feeling". This will be done only in a realm where the subjective and the objective meet, or rather, where the subjective approaches and becomes at one with the objective. A poem is a spontaneous creation of a man in such a state. It is something which naturally comes out of this realm, and not the result of forced will or logical thinking.

The identification of the self and the external object, of course, is an illogical act of intuition and is done in an instant of time. It is, from the poet's point of view, an instantaneous perception of hidden reality. Bashō emphasizes this as Dohō records his words and explains them:

On composing *haiku* the Master once commented: "If you get a flash of insight into an object, put it into words before it fades away in your mind." He also said: "Toss out the feeling to the surface of your poem." These teachings mean that one should set his poetic feeling into form instantly after he gets into the realm, before the feeling cools off. In composing *haiku* there are two ways: "becoming" and "making". When a poet who has always been assiduous in pursuit of his aim applies himself to an external object, the color of his mind naturally becomes a poem. In the case of a poet who has not done so, nothing in him will become a poem; he, consequently, has to make out a poem through the act of his personal will.[8]

Suggesting that poetic creation is a momentary act of inspiration, Bashō advises that a poet should never miss the inspired moment. The moment is when the poet "gets a flash of insight into an object", a moment of communion between the

8   *Ibid.*, 164.

subjective and the objective. A poem is a result of the poet's unconscious act and not of his will; a poet does not "make" a poem, – something in him naturally "becomes" a poem. The inspired moment, however, does not come upon anyone at any moment; each poet should constantly strive to make it come through meditation and concentration. Yet, when the moment comes, the poet's mind is devoid of personal will; it is completely transparent, whereupon an external object dyes it in its own color and creates a beautiful picture. Bashō uses the term "*haiku* without other thoughts" in describing the ideal stage of poetic achievement.[9] Evidently he refers to a state of mind in which there is no impure element, no personal element of the poet which would stain the whiteness of his soul at the moment.

This concept seems to come close to Baudelaire's idea of "correspondence".[10] Baudelaire, in revolt against the scientific spirit of his time, put forth his mystical method of cognition in his well-known poem, "Correspondences". Instead of recognizing an external existence through one's subjective awareness, the French poet proposes to wander among symbols of nature and have close communion with it. A scientific analysis can only present an object as an incomplete accumulation of parts; Baudelaire's method enables one to feel an object in its entity, in a superhuman world of harmony. The aspects of correspondence which he points out in "Correspondences" are two: a correspondence between man and nature, and that between different human senses. Both aspects seem to exist in Bashō's concept of poetry. The first we have already seen, and we shall discuss the second a little later.

Bashō's mode of perception is thus quite different from that of science, but it also shows a departure from that of traditional Japanese poetry. Indeed, classical Japanese poetry is filled with communion between man and nature, yet in it man momentarily identifies himself with nature in order to express

[9]  *Ibid.*, 181.
[10]  Cf. Yoshie Okazaki, "Banbutsu kōkan" (Correspondences), *Okazaki Yoshie chosaku-shū*, VI, 53-83.

his emotion. *Waka* poets "express their emotions through the objects they see and hear," as a famous Japanese statement on the nature of poetry goes. In Bashō's view, however, external reality is the primary element in poetic creation. We have already seen how Bashō advised a poet to negate his personal will in order to perceive the "delicate life" of a natural object. He remarks in another passage: "Do not neglect natural objects at any time."[11] At the root of his thinking lies the idea: "When we observe them calmly, we notice that all things have their fulfilment."[12] A pine tree lives its own life, a bamboo fulfils its own destiny; a pine never tries to become a bamboo, or a bamboo does not envy the life of a pine. A poet, therefore, should learn from a pine things about a pine, and from a bamboo things about a bamboo. Bashō remarks, as recorded by Dohō:

The Master said: "Changes in nature are said to be the seed of poetic spirit. Calm things show the aspects of permanence. Active things reveal the changes. Unless a poet records each change at that very moment, he will never be able to record it. By the word "record" I mean to record by perceiving or hearing. Blossoms fly, leaves fall, they lie scattered on the ground; unless a poet perceives or hears these phenomena within the phenomena, he will never succeed in recording them in his heart."[13]

The idea embodied in the first half of this passage is little different from that of *waka*, but the second half is typical of *haiku*. Whereas *waka* poets would sing of falling blossoms to mourn over their lost love, Bashō thinks that a phenomenon must be seen within the phenomenon and not from a human point of view. In *haiku*, or at least in the *haiku* of the Bashō school, we do not find a personal emotion expressed as we do in *waka* or in Western poetry in general.

Apparently, this view of poetry was rooted in Bashō's attitude toward life. Or, perhaps, Bashō's devotion to poetry motivated his attitude toward life; for, Bashō's view of life is what we may call an aesthetic view. He looks at life in the

[11] *Sanzōshi, SH,* 182.
[12] "Minomushi batsu", *BI,* 614.
[13] *Sanzōshi, SH,* 164.

same manner as one looks at a work of art. We have noted that Bashō discouraged the intrusion of a personal emotion into creative process. In fact he went a step farther; he proposed to minimize the activity of a personal emotion in actual life as well. Personal emotions are difficult to get rid of when we get ourselves involved in the struggles of life; Bashō suggests that we can avoid the involvement if we view our life from an aesthetic distance. We do not try to change our society; we only change our attitude toward society, we face our society in the same manner as we see a painting, hear music, or read a poem. We enjoy a story of war since we are not in a war ourselves; we shall enjoy our life more, in Bashō's view, if we do not follow the utilitarian ways of life. Bashō's ideal life is, in his words, "to enjoy life by being indifferent to worldly interests, by forgetting whether one is young or old". He continues:

A foolish man has many things to worry about. Those who are troubled with sinful desires and become expert in some art or another are persons with a strong sense of right and wrong. But some who make art the source of their livelihood rouse their hearts in anger in the hell of greed and drown themselves in a small ditch; they are unable to keep their art alive.[14]

One way to transcend worldly involvements is to become a poet – a *haiku* poet. Bashō says: "The *haiku* is like a fireplace in summer or a fan in winter. Contrary to the popular needs, it has no immediate utility."[15]

Of course a poet, being a man also, cannot be completely detached from worldly concerns; he has to eat, wear clothes, live in a house. He may do all these things, yet the important thing is not to be bothered with a desire to possess more than enough. This is a significant point at which Bashō's "poetic spirit" differs from hermitism or asceticism. A hermit or an ascetic imposes seclusion or abstinence upon himself. Bashō, on the other hand, does not reject the things of the world; he only advises us to look at them from a distance, without com-

[14] "Heikan no setsu", *BI*, 627.
[15] "Saimon no ji", *BI*, 633.

mitting ourselves to them. The *haiku* poet's attitude toward life is that of a by-stander. A man with an impulsive temperament or a strong desire will find it difficult to become a *haiku* poet; perhaps such a man would better go to religion in order to attain serenity of mind. The *haiku* requires a passive, leisurely personality by its very nature.

In *haiku*, therefore, there is no passionate emotion, no strong sentiment. There is only the shadow of an emotion, or a vague mood. Instead of joy, there is a formless atmosphere arising from happiness; instead of grief, there is a mood vaguely suggesting quiet resignation. There is, for instance, a famous farewell poem which Bashō composed upon leaving for a distant journey:

> Spring is going...
> Birds weep, and the eyes of fish
> are filled with tears.[16]

A long journey through rural areas of northern Japan was ahead of him, and he was old, sickly, and not sure of his safe return. But there is no personal grief in the poem. Bashō's sentiment is depersonalized. It is spring that goes; it is birds and fish that weep. There is no acute pain; there is only a vague sadness which fills nature. To take another example, here is a poem which Bashō wrote as he mourned over his disciple's death:

> In the autumn wind
> lies, sorrowfully broken,
> a mulberry stick.[17]

Compare this with another poem by Bashō which describes dead grass in winter:

> All flowers are dead.
> Only a sorrow lies, with
> the grass-seeds.[18]

---

[16] *Oku no hosomichi*, *BI*, 587.
[17] *Oi nikki*, *BI*, 52.
[18] *Tomaribune-shū*, *BI*, 79.

It is roughly the same mood that prevails over these two poems, although the occasions would have evoked widely different emotions in an ordinary person. It was not that Bashō was inhuman; he was only "unhuman". This element becomes more obvious in his better poems:

> Quietness...
> The cicadas' voice
> penetrates the rocks.[19]

> The rough sea...
> Far over Sado Isle, extends
> the Milky Way.[20]

> Gathering the rains
> of June, how swiftly flows
> the Mogami River![21]

In these pieces there is little trace of the emotion which the poet originally had on each occasion. All that we get is the feeling of the quiet, the vast, or the swift. The poet never says happy or sad, wonderful or disgusting. He only crystalizes the feeling of nature. Nature has no personal emotion, but it has life. The best of Bashō's *haiku* catch this life through certain moods which surround it.

This quality at once explains the two fundamental pre-requisites of *haiku* which are observed even today: the seventeen syllable form, and the rule requiring a word suggestive of a season. The *haiku* is an extremely short poem, normally consisting of three lines with five, seven and five syllables each. The *waka* is short, too, but it is still long enough to express one's emotion in the form of a statement. The *haiku* does not permit the poet either to explain, to describe, or to state; an idea, or a sentiment, will never be fully put forth within the space of seventeen syllables. This is a perfect medium for the *haiku* poet who avoids a systematic presentation of an idea or emotion; it requires him to depersonalize his emotion, if he

[19] *Oku no hosomichi, BI* 595.
[20] *Kanjinchō, BI*, 48.
[21] *Oku no hosomichi, BI*, 595.

ever has one, through an object in nature. Here comes in the second prerequisite of *haiku*, that a *haiku* must contain a word referring to a season of the year. A personal sentiment, if any, will become a thing of nature in the poem. Furthermore, unlike a *waka* poet, the *haiku* writer cannot go through a process in which he starts with his own feeling and then finds an object which will best express that feeling; his best "objective correlative" may not happen to be a thing related to a season. The *haiku* poet must begin with a natural object or objects outside of himself; even though he has an emotion in himself, he has to submerge it in an outside object, whereupon a certain mood arises which would vaguely suggest the original feeling but never set it in the foreground of the poem.

It is relevant, in this connection, to observe the historical development of Japanese poetry and the origin of the *haiku* form. When the earliest anthology of Japanese poetry was compiled in the eighth century, there were two verse-forms: the *waka* with thirty-one syllables and the *chōka* with an indefinite number of syllables. After the latter form became obsolete, the former went a downward way as it lost freshness and vitality. In the tenth and eleventh centuries the *waka* was a plaything in the court circles, who, except for a few genuine poets, used the form to display their wit or scholarship, to express their over-sentimental love or sense of life's transience. Some time around 1200 a reaction set in; the new poets, still using the *waka* form, turned from the poetry of intellect to that of mood, from the verse of statement to that of suggestion. In contrast with an ordinary Japanese poem which follows the usual sentence structure ending with the predicate verb, the poet of this time often ended his poem with a noun, leaving out the predicate verb; the reader was expected to supply the verb by himself, to complete the poem in his own imagination. The poet, instead of composing a self-contained entity, created a poem which left so many things unsaid that the reader felt need to supplement the poem by creating another poem by himself. The linked verse stemmed from this tradition; one set of linked verse was a joint product of several poets who supplemented each other's imagination and completed each other's work. What they aimed at was a creation of some unique mood, delicate, graceful and harmonious. Presently, the opening stanza of linked verse became independent and took the form of what we now call *haiku*. The independence of *haiku* from linked verse marked a revolution in the history of Japanese verse. What sort of revolution it was, or how the *haiku* differed from the *waka* in mood, will be further discussed later in this chapter, in connection with "lightness". Let it suffice here to note that the *haiku* form was not a casual invention of a genius but an offspring of an age-long tradition.

Bashō, however, did not talk much about the rules of *haiku* form or of a season word, nor did he strictly prohibit a departure from them. In fact he himself composed many poems with more than seventeen syllables, as well as a few poems with no season word. On the other hand, there were certain ideas on verse-writing which Bashō positively insisted on. Chief among them were *sabi*, *shiori*, *hosomi*, "inspiration", "fragrance", "reverberation", "reflection", and "lightness". They are different from each other, as the terms are different. But they have one thing in common, the "poetic spirit". The first three and "lightness" designate certain attitudes toward life, and, as we shall see presently, they all stem from the same basic view of life that underlies the poetic spirit. The remaining four are concerned with the technique of *haiku* composition; they make clear certain ways in which the poetic spirit can be made manifest in a poem.

The word *sabi* stems from an adjective *sabishi*, which literally means "lonely" or "desolate". Bashō himself never used the term *sabi* in his writing, but he did use *sabishi*. One of the instances appears in a poem which he wrote while living alone at a lonely temple:

> My sorrowful soul...
> Make it feel more lonesome,
> you, a cuckoo.[22]

[22]   *Saga nikki*, BI, 606.

Sorrow is a personal emotion, while loneliness, in this context, is an impersonal mood existent in a cuckoo's voice. The poet, as it were, wants the purification of his soul, the transformation of the personal into the impersonal. *Sabi* seems to imply such an impersonal emotion – a mood. It is not personal loneliness, but a lonely mood latent in nature. The same point is suggested in Kyorai's well-known passage on *sabi*:

*Sabi* refers to the color of a poem. It does not mean the emotion of loneliness embodied in the poem. *Sabi* is like what we feel about an aged man, whether he fights in battlefield wearing a suit of armor, or attends a banquet with a brocade garment on. *Sabi* may lie either in a gay poem or in a tranquil one. I shall quote a poem for illustration:

> Under the blossoms
> two watchmen talk, with their white
> heads together.

The Master said that the *sabi* color was very well expressed in this poem.[23]

Kyorai, learning from Bashō, argues that *sabi* lies not in the substance or technique but in the "color" of a poem. "Color" seems to mean the quality of the mood which the poem embodies. The poem may deal with a lively party scene or a quiet country life; but the materials do not much matter, the important thing is the atmosphere which permeates the poem. A poet may, for example, depict lovely cherry-blossoms in full bloom, yet the "color" of his poem may be that of *sabi* because the poem also presents two aged men quietly talking under the blossoms. By contrasting white hair with pink blossoms, the poet suggests the coming fall of the blossoms, a destiny for both men and the objects of nature. But the poem by no means laments over the mutability of life; it simply describes a scene, out of which arises a mood ambiguously pointing toward sadness or loneliness. Bashō's way of saying it is that the poem has the color of *sabi*.

*Sabi*, then, is a poetic mood vaguely pointing toward a certain view of life. This view of life is called *wabi*. *Wabi*

[23]   *Kyorai shō, SH,* 276-277.

originally meant "sadness of poverty". But gradually it came
to mean an attitude toward life, with which one tried to
resign himself to straitened living and to find peace and serenity of mind even under such circumstances. People considered sadness as an unavoidable condition of living in this
world; they endeavored to overcome it by getting themselves
accustomed to the inconveniences of life. Bashō liked to
travel, primarily for this reason. He writes:

My straw hat was worn out by rain on the way, and my robe too
was crumpled up through the storms I had met here and there. My
appearance was so extremely shabby that even I myself felt a little
sad. It just occurred to me that many years ago a gifted comic-
verse writer had traveled in this province. Thereupon I too composed a comic *haiku*:

> In the wintry gust
> I wander, like Chikusai
> the comic poet.[24]

Here again the poet subdues his grief by looking at himself
from a distance. His situation is sad enough from an ordinary
man's point of view; he himself says he felt sad. But he steps
backwards from vital feelings of life, he looks at his own situation as if it were someone else's; then he realizes that the
situation is not sad but even a little humorous. Such an attitude is the later implication of *wabi*. *Sabi*, primarily an aesthetic concept, is closely associated with *wabi*, a philosophical
idea. *Sabi*, as we have observed, is not an emotion but an
impersonal mood; the process of depersonalization is done
through *wabi*, in which the poet looks at himself and his emotion from a distance, as if looking at some natural object.
Personal sorrow becomes universal loneliness; sadness over
transiency of life becomes a vague mood arising from it.

Of *shiori* Kyorai has repeatedly said: "*Shiori* in poetry does
not mean a poem with the feeling of pity",[25] "*shiori* and a
poem with the feeling of pity are different",[26] and so forth.

---

[24] *Fuyu no hi, BI*, 75.
[25] *Kyorai shō, SH*, 277.
[26] "Kyoshi no monnan ni kotauru no ben", *SH*, 420.

This implies that *shiori* and pity are fairly close, and that the people of his time often confused the two. The difference, according to Kyorai, is that *shiori* does not lie in the topic or diction or material of the poem while pity does. "*Shiori*", writes Kyorai, "lies in the form of a poem."[27] And he says elsewhere: "*Shiori* is a suggested feeling."[28] From these comments we may gather that *shiori* is a certain mood arising from the poem itself rather than from the ingredients of the poem, and that it is somewhat close to pity but differs from it in that it is not a personal feeling. The complex meaning of *shiori* may be traced back to its double origin. The term *shiori* stems from a verb *shioru*, which means "to bend" or "to be flexible". Originally, therefore, *shiori* seems to have been used in describing a poem which is not stiff or straightforward in expression but is flexible in meaning and allows several levels of interpretation. Yet it so happened that there was another verb *shioru*, written differently and declined differently but pronounced the same, describing a withered flower or a frustrated man. This implication seems to have found its way into the noun *shiori* and combined itself with the original meaning of the term. Thus *shiori*, in its later usage, describes a poem which allows several levels of meaning all of which have the common undertone of sadness – if we understand sadness to be an impersonal mood as distinct from pity which is a personal feeling. A poem of pity would contain an intense, personal emotion as we often see in a dirge or elegy. A poem of *shiori*, on the other hand, would embody an indefinable, ambiguous mood surrounding the feeling of pity; the reader would wonder, for example, whether the poem is about a particular person's death, or about man's mortality in general, or about the passing of summer. The ambiguity of meaning widens the scope of the poem; it elevates a personal feeling to the universal. Kyorai quotes a poem which Bashō thought had the quality of *shiori*:

[27] *Kyorai shō, SH*, 277.
[28] "Kyoshi no monnan ni kotauru no ben", *SH*, 420.

The Ten Dumplings
have become smaller too.
The autumn wind...[29]

The Ten Dumplings, so called because they are sold in units of
ten by stringing them together, are a special product of a small
mountain village in central Japan. It is autumn; travelers
have become fewer and fewer. The villagers, who make their
living by selling dumplings to travelers, are now in a straitened
state; their dumplings, as a consequence, have become smaller. The mood which prevails over the poem is what we may
call sadness. But, we ask, what is the sadness directed toward?
Toward the local villagers? Toward the fate of mankind,
represented by the villagers? Toward the poet himself, the
lonely traveler? Toward the summer that has gone? Or toward both man and nature that must change with time? The
word "too" and the verbless last line leave the whole meaning
ambiguous; nevertheless the mood which comes out of it gives
us a uniform impression of sadness. The feeling of pity, which
the poet originally felt toward the villagers, is universalized by
the ambiguity which the poem embodies. While the mood of
*sabi* is based on a certain philosophical attitude, that of *shiori*
comes out of the ambiguity in meaning. Both of these moods
have a certain, almost identical undertone, although, perhaps, *shiori* has a greater implication of sadness than of loneliness.

Zeami also had a notion similar to *shiori* and expressed it in
a similar term: we remember his metaphor of a withering
flower in describing the effect of a superb *nō* performance.
His *shiori*, however, seems to differ from Bashō's in two main
respects. First, it strictly follows the implication of our second
verb *shioru*, which means "to wither". Zeami's idea, consequently, does not imply flexibility or ambiguity. Secondly,
Zeami's *shiori* always seems to have its contrast in the background: behind *shiori* there lingers graceful, flowering beauty.
We see a blooming flower in a withering one, blossoms on a

---

[29]   *Kyorai shō, SH*, 277.

dead tree. We recognize no such double image in Bashō's
*shiori*. A dead tree is a dead tree; it is beautiful because it has
followed its destiny to the end.

*Hosomi*, literally meaning "slenderness", seems to mean the
delicacy of sentiment lying in the depth of a poem. Kyorai
says: "*Hosomi* is not found in a feeble poem." Then he continues: "*Hosomi* lies in the feeling of a poem." The poem he
cites for illustration is:

> I wonder whether
> seabirds too are asleep
> on Lake Yogo tonight.[30]

The poet is trying to sleep under a thin quilt in a cold winter
night at a certain lakeside village. Suddenly he hears a
seabird's cry. At once he compares himself with the seabird,
and wonders if the seabirds on the lake are too cold to go to
sleep. The poet buries himself in an external object with
delicate sensitivity; this is *hosomi*. It is, as it were, a fine vibration of the poet's heart in response to the smallest stimulus in
nature. *Hosomi* is a sensitive working of the heart which penetrates into the innermost nature of things. It is subtle but not
feeble; it has a power coming from the poet's mind concen-
trated on the smallest phenomenon in nature. Anyone can
catch crude emotions such as anger or jealousy, yet it requires
utmost sensitivity to grasp a formless mood which surrounds
the life of a natural object.

*Hosomi* is referred to by Bashō in another instance, when he
commented on a poem by one of his disciples:

> The monkey's shriek
> is hoarse, his teeth white.
> Over the peak, the moon.

Bashō criticized the poet for his excessive desire to create an
unusual scene, and himself composed a *haiku* for the sake of
contrast:

[30]   *Ibid.*, 277.

A salted sea-bream,
showing its teeth, lies chilly
at the fish shop.[31]

The writer of the first poem has not put himself in the monkey's position; he is standing a little distance away from the
monkey and listening to his shriek. But Bashō has set himself
within the object – a sea-bream. Just as the writer of the seabird poem can feel what the seabirds feel, Bashō feels chilly
as the salted fish feels chilly at a fish shop in winter. The whiteness of the fish's exposed teeth has caused a delicate vibration
of the the poet's heart, establishing a slender but firm relation
between the fish and the poet. This quality is explained as
*hosomi*.

"Inspiration" refers to an instantaneous insight into the
hidden nature of things. Bashō repeatedly taught his disciples
not to miss an inspired moment in composing a poem. "If you
get a flash of insight into an object", we have already heard
him say, "put it into words before it fades away in your mind".
"Even though a poet may get a glimpse at the real nature of
things", Dohō explains, "he may either nourish his perception
or kill it. If he kills his perception, his poem will not have life.
The Master once taught that a poet should compose a poem
with the force of his inspiration."[32] Bashō advises that a flash
of insight should be crystalized into a *haiku* before any impure
element gets in the way. Dohō records:

The Master said: "A poet should discipline himself every day.
When he sits at a poetry contest, he should be able to make up a
poem instantly after his turn comes; there should be no lapse of
time between him and the writing desk. If the poet quickly puts
into words what he has just felt, he will have nothing to hesitate
about. The manuscript of a poem is no better than a trash paper
when it is finished and is taken down from the writing desk."
This was the Master's strict teaching. At another time he said:
"Composition of a poem must be done in an instant, like a woodcutter felling a huge tree or a swordsman leaping at a dangerous
enemy. It is also like cutting a ripe watermelon with a sharp knife,

[31]　Fūshi, *Haikai jiteiki* (1750's). Quoted in *Bashō kōza*, III, 8.
[32]　*Sanzōshi, SH*, 163.

or like taking a large bite at a pear. Consider all thirty-six poems as light verse." All these words show the Master's attempt to remove personal will from the artist's work.[33]

"Inspiration" does not come from the Muse; it comes from the poet's constant training and discipline. When it arrives, it arrives in an instant. The poet should catch the inspired moment and put his experience into words on the spot. What is important is the inspiration of the moment, and not the arrangement of the words as they are put down on a piece of paper. The manuscript of a poem is in itself nothing more than a trash paper; a poem is alive only when it is in the stage of being composed or read on a writing desk. Therefore, once the poem is finished at the inspired moment, do not change words from one to another. Compose the whole set of thirty-six poems in a light mood – that is, not in a grave mood of a philosophical thinker. "Inspiration" is intuitive, and not cogitative. It is not something which the poet wrings out of himself by effort. The poet's effort should be toward the direction of making it possible for such a moment of "inspiration" to visit upon him.

Bashō rejects artifice on the same ground. Artifice kills "inspiration"; it is merely an intellectual play, without an intuitive insight into nature. Bashō calls it "a craftsman's disease". "Let a little boy compose *haiku*", says he. "A beginner's poem always has something promising."[34] Often the poet's too eager effort to write a good poem does harm to his work, because his personal will tends to show in the foreground of the poem. A good *haiku* cannot be written merely by a long verse-writing experience or by wide knowledge of the technique of *haiku*. For this reason, "some who have been practising *haiku* for many years are slower in knowing true *haiku* than others who are new in *haiku* but who have been expert in other arts", Bashō says.[35] Here again we see Bashō's idea that all arts are the same in spirit and that this spirit is

---

[33]   *Ibid.*, 163.
[34]   *Ibid.*, 163.
[35]   *Ibid.*, 163.

the most important element in *haiku*-writing as well as in other arts.

"Fragrance", "reverberation" and "reflection" are the main principles which rule the relation between parts of a poem. These terms are often used in linked verse, but they are basic ideas in *haiku*-writing too. Among them "fragrance" is the oldest idea in Japanese aesthetics, frequently used in the *waka* tradition. "Fragrance" means "fragrance of sentiment", some vague quality rising out of a mood and appealing to human senses. Bashō seems to have believed that different parts of a poem should be related to one another by "fragrance", forming an atmospheric harmony rather than logical coherence as a whole. Dohō points out some examples in linked verse:

> How bothersome
> are the innumerable names
> of spring flowers!

> A butterfly, slapped,
> awakes out of its sleep.

The scene of the second stanza was conceived in harmony with the first, as its writer felt the fragrance of mind in the expression "bothersome" and visualized a butterfly flying up in alarm.[36]

The first stanza describes the loveliness of spring flowers: all flowers are so beautifully blooming that it is bothersome to remember them by different names. Yet the expression "bothersome" vaguely suggests a certain quality of mood – somewhat unsettled, faintly uneasy, as if something is fluttering in the corner of a beautiful landscape. The second stanza takes over this "fragrance" of mood suggested in the first stanza and introduces the image of a fluttering butterfly. The relation between the two stanzas, therefore, is "fragrance".

Dohō has many linked *haiku* which illustrate the principle of "fragrance", but we shall take just one more example:

> A weasel sharply squeaks
> somewhere behind the shelves.

---

[36] *Ibid.*, 174.

> Tall bloom-plants,
> sewn by no one, grow
> thickly in the yard.

The writer of the second stanza could faintly hear a desolate fragrance between the lines of the first stanza and added the scene of a dilapidated house with wild bloom-plants heavily growing in the yard.[37]

The first stanza has the "fragrance" of a lonely mood: the squeak of a weasel suggests a desolate house in remote wilderness. This particular quality that permeates the mood of the first stanza is strengthened by the image of densely growing bloom-plants in the second. The second stanza follows the first, but again by no logical necessity; it is only a peculiar "fragrance" that unites the two.

"Reverberation" implies a relation of two parts in a poem in which the mood of one part reverberates in the other. Kyorai explains:

Reverberation in poetry may be compared to the case of two objects in which as soon as the one is hit the other reverberates from it. For instance:

> On the long porch
> a silver-glazed cup
> is smashed to pieces.

> Watch the long, slender sword
> he is about to draw!

The Master taught me with this example, himself imitating the action of flinging a cup in his right hand and of preparing to draw a sword in his left.[38]

The first stanza describes a tense scene in which a fierce quarrel has begun among swordsmen at a banquet, whereupon one of them in anger smashed his wine cup on the porch. The poet of the second stanza heard the vibration of this mood and composed a stanza which would vibrate with the first: in the second stanza the mood is even tenser as two warriors prepare to fight. Here is another example quoted by Dohō:

---

[37] *Ibid.*, 176.
[38] *Kyorai shō, SH,* 273.

> In the blue sky
> dimly hangs the moon
> as the day breaks.

> The first frost has fallen
> at Hira, by the autumn lake.

The writer of the second stanza was inspired by the first line of the first stanza and created a clear, fresh, magnificent scene with the autumn lake and the first frost at Hira.[39]

The first stanza presents a beautiful mood with a wan morning moon, but there is one image, the blue sky, which suggests the feeling of magnitude. This causes a reverberation in the second stanza and introduces the magnificent scene of a large lake extending into an infinite distance in the chilly autumn air. "Reverberation," then, is like "fragrance" in its function; it relates one part of a poem to another by a certain quality of mood. Yet, whereas "fragrance" accompanies a calm, elegant mood, "reverberation" appears only when the mood is of tension, excitement, grandeur or magnitude. Such a mood, as it were, is so forceful that it causes an echo in a stanza that follows.

As for "reflection", Bashō's own comment is recorded:

> Men are cutting the brushwood
> by a grassy path on the peak.

> In the dense pine-wood
> on the leftside mountain
> is the Temple of Kaya.

The Master said: "In view of the reflection from the line 'Men are cutting the brushwood,' it would be better to change the opening line of the second stanza to 'It is hailing....'"[40]

The force of the first line in the first stanza is strong, rough and coarse. But "In the dense pine-wood" implies a silent, calm atmosphere. So Bashō thought that the mood of the second stanza did not "reflect" that of the first, and advised to change the line to "It is hailing ...", which would correspond to the roughness of the mood in the first stanza. "Reflection", again

---

[39] *Sanzōshi, SH*, 175.
[40] "Sanchō sangin hyōgo", *BI*, 553.

like "fragrance" or "reverberation", is the reflection of a mood between two different parts of a poem creating a harmony as a whole. Its basic difference from "fragrance" or "reverberation" is that "reflection" can be applied to any mood, quiet or violent.

The concepts of "fragrance", "reverberation" and "reflection" show that in *haiku* the relation between parts is based on a vague feeling of similarity in mood. In *haiku* it is quite possible to bring together two widely different things and still create some strange yet harmonious mood as a whole. The two things may have nothing in common to ordinary eyes, but the imaginative union of the two may create an unusually beautiful fragrance, reverberation or reflection. One of the consequences of this unique idea is the merging of different senses in *haiku*. The very fact that Bashō used such terms as "fragrance", "reverberation" or "reflection" in denoting a mood suggests his belief in the interrelatedness of the five senses; from an ordinary point of view a mood would have no smell, no sound, no color. Bashō saw an experience in its total impact; odor, sound and color were one to him. Hence examples of synesthesia are abundant in his work. Among his poems which imply a correspondence between sound and color are:

> As evening has come
> on the sea, wild ducks' cry
> is faintly white.[41]

> Quietness...
> On the wall, where hangs a painting,
> a grasshopper chirps.[42]

The blending of vision and the sense of temperature is seen in such poems as:

> Onions lie
> washed all in white.
> How chilly it is![43]

[41]  *Nozarashi kikō, BI,* 88.
[42]  *Bashō-ō shōsoku-shū, BI,* 56.
[43]  *Infutagi, BI,* 86.

> The autumn wind
> whiter than the rocks of
> the Rock Mountain...[44]

Vision and odor are fused in these poems:

> Scent of orchids...
> It perfumes the wings
> of a butterfly.[45]

> Their fragrance
> is whiter than peach-blossoms:
> the daffodils.[46]

The correspondence between sound and smell is shown in the
following poems:

> The wind fragrantly
> sounds, as if to praise
> the pines and cedars.[47]

> The rippling waves...
> They beat time, with the fragrance
> of the breeze.[48]

In addition to these, there are many poems in which synesthesia is implied. They juxtapose two different human
senses in such a way that a strange fusion of the two will take
place. Some of the best poems by Bashō belong to this category:

> Quietly, quietly,
> yellow flowers fall to the ground.
> The sound of the rapids...[49]

> The chrysanthemum smell...
> In the old town of Nara
> many ancient Buddhas.[50]

[44]   *Oku no hosomichi*, *BI*, 599.
[45]   *Bashō-ō shinseki-shū*, *BI*, 53.
[46]   *Oi nikki*, *BI*, 80.
[47]   *Ibid.*, 38.
[48]   *Ibid.*, 38.
[49]   *Areno*, *BI*, 23.
[50]   *Oi nikki*, *BI*, 70.

A cuckoo's cry...
The moonbeams are leaking
through the thick bamboos.[51]

Yellow flowers and the sound of water, the fragrance of chry-
santhemums and old Buddhist images, a cuckoo's cry and the
moonbeams – there is no immediate relation between the two
that constitute these pairs; yet the poet brings the two together – by the principle of "fragrance", "reverberation" or
"reflection" – and creates a uniquely harmonious mood on the
whole. The *haiku* often contains several things contradictory to
each other; but still it has an atmospheric unity, the "poetic
spirit" permeating its heterogeneous materials. This is the
point at which the "correspondence" in *haiku* differs from its
counterpart in French symbolist poetry. French symbolists
deliberately try to unite two disparate objects and create the
beauty of artifice; their beauty is the perfume of "amber,
musk, benjamin and incense" – strong, sensual, artificial,
sophisticated, often decadent and even abnormal. The beauty
springing out of Bashō's "correspondence" is like the fragrance of a chrysanthemum or orchid – faint, natural, simple,
primitive, and never extravagant or shocking. This, of course,
stems from his attitude toward life, from his "poetic spirit",
which we have already discussed.

The attitude which tries to accept all things as they are in
life came to form another aesthetic concept, "lightness", in
Bashō. As he grew old Bashō emphasized this notion so much
that it almost appeared as if he thought it the highest ideal
of *haiku*. "By all means endeavor to produce lightness", he
says to one of his disciples, "and tell this to your friends too".[52]
"I was delighted", he says to another, "to find that, among
other improvements, lightness has come to prevail in your
poetry in general".[53] As for the nature of "lightness", there is
an interesting dialogue in Kyorai's writings:

A certain man asked about the new flavor of *haiku*. The Master

---

[51]  *Saga nikki*, *BI*, 605.
[52]  Bashō's letter to Sanpū, June 24, 1694. *Bashō kōza*, VII, 291.
[53]  Bashō's letter to Dohō, September 23, 1694. *Ibid.*, 320.

said: "Do not take duck soup; sip fragrant vegetable soup instead."
The man inquired: "How could vegetable soup be compared to
duck soup?" The Master smiled and gave no answer. As I was
sitting by, I said to the man: "It is no wonder that you should not
be tired of duck soup. I have never seen you eating it. You crave
for it day and night." The Master said: "Do not stop even for a
moment. If you do, your poetry will become heavy."[54]

"Lightness" is a beauty found in common, everyday things.
It is not gorgeous but plain, not sophisticated but naive, not
greasy but faintly fragrant. It is a simple beauty, as Bashō
says elsewhere: "When you compose a poem, be simple and
bold ..."[55] It is free of sentimentalism, as he criticizes a certain poem for being sweet.[56] It is a beauty of innocence, as he
says: "Simply observe what children do."[57] It is also "shallow", as he says: "The style I have in mind resembles a shallow sand-bed river. Both the form and content of a poem
should be light."[58] "Shallow" does not imply lack of depth
in meaning. Poetry is compared to the pure water flowing in a
shallow sand-bed river; it is transparent, smooth, and not
stagnant. A "shallow" or "light" poem, in other words, is
devoid of any intent to teach philosophical ideas or to indulge
in deep emotions. That "lightness" does not connote the
shallowness of thought or feeling is obvious in the second half
of Kyorai's passage as quoted above. Only those who have
tasted duck soup may properly appreciate the flavor of vegetable soup; only those who can deeply feel may attain the
stage of transcendental "lightness". The relation between
"lightness" and "heaviness" is not antithetical but dialectical.
  The nature of "lightness" is further clarified as Bashō men-
tions an actual example. It is, as cited by Dohō:

> Under the trees
> soup, fish salad, and all,
> in cherry-blossoms.

[54]   "Fugyoku ate ronsho", (1695), *Kyorai shō; Sanzōshi; Tabine-ron*, 226.
[55]   *Ibid.*, 226.
[56]   *Kyorai shō, SH*, 252.
[57]   *Tabine-ron, SH*, 233.
[58]   "Betsuzashiki jo", *Shōmon haikai zenshū*, 529.

When this poem was composed, the Master said: "This has a flavor of blossom-viewing poetry in the mood of lightness."[59]

Cherry-blossom viewing, of course, had been a common poetic theme since ancient times. But this *haiku* differs from traditional blossom-viewing poems because it does not praise the loveliness of blossoms nor mourn over the passing of spring, but introduces a down-to-earth subject, food. The mood which comes out of a scene where beautiful blossoms are falling on soup and fish salad is "lightness".

Thus "lightness", implying naivete and familiarity in style as well as in subject-matter, makes a distinct departure from the tradition of classical Japanese literature. In fact Dohō writes:

Chinese verse, *waka*, linked verse and *haiku* are all poetry. Yet *haiku* covers all the areas of life, including the things which have not been treated in the other three.[60]

Chinese poetry, *waka* and linked verse aim at the creation of heroic or elegant beauty; naturally their materials are limited. Yet *haiku*, with its "lightness", accepts all things for its material – a muddy crow, a bird's dropping, or even horse-dung. The beauty of *haiku* is that of the "poetic spirit" which discovers delicate workings of the universal energy in all things of life. If one looks at things with the "poetic spirit", even the pettiest, humblest things will become subjects of poetry as precious as the blossoms and the moon. The *haiku* poet may use colloquialism too, which was a taboo in classical Chinese and Japanese poetry. "One use of *haiku*", says Bashō, "is to correct colloquialism."[61] A vernacular word, when it is used in *haiku*, is no longer crude or indecent; it is "corrected", it is elevated to the poetic level. Thus the realm of *haiku*, both in subject-matter and in language, is as broad as the whole range of human life.

A light mood as a distinguishing element of the *haiku* is

[59]   *Sanzōshi, SH*, 169.
[60]   *Ibid.*, 155.
[61]   *Ibid.*, 182.

re-emphasized by Dohō when he says: "a willow tree in the spring rain completely belongs to the world of linked verse. A crow digging up mud-snails is an exclusive property of *haiku* poets." Indeed we cannot imagine a graceful linked verse writer watching a dirty crow digging the muddy rice-paddy. A *haiku* poet, on the other hand, can write a poem like:

> In the rain of June
> let us go and see the floating
> nest of a little grebe.[62]

No ordinary adult would be tempted to go out in the rain just to see a grebe's nest on the pond. But the poet Bashō, with almost a childlike innocence, enjoys doing so. "Let us go and see" successfully conveys the lightheartedness of the poet, which is in the center of the poem's mood.

The principle of "lightness" results in another characteristic of *haiku*, humor. The world of man is full of contradictions and struggles, and one is often provoked, angry and desperate. A *haiku* poet, however, looks at them from a distance, with the sympathy of a man who has calmly given up fighting. Life is a tragedy to those who feel, but is a comedy to those who stop and think. When the *haiku* poet leisurely watches other people without being involved in their emotions, a smile forms in his face, humor emerges in his work. For instance:

> Noiselessly
> a peasant makes straw sandals
> in the moonlight,
>
> when a neighbor wakes to shake off
> the fleas in early autumn.[63]

The first stanza depicts a poor farmhouse scene. The peasant, unable to live on his daytime work alone, makes straw sandals late at night; he works in the moonlight outdoors to save lighting oil, yet he has to be cautious not to disturb sleeping neighbors. The second stanza, while carrying on the modest

---

[62]    *Ibid.*, 155.
[63]    *Ibid.*, 175.

village scene, introduces a streak of humor by describing a neighbor awakened by fleas and coming out of his shack to shake them off. The poet shows no indignation or sentimentality at the poor peasant life; he only watches it understandingly and smilingly.

The *haiku*, then, was for Bashō the way to salvation. As he recalls, there were times when he craved for an official post or wanted to become a monk, yet he failed in both and hung to the thin string of *haiku*.[64] Bashō refused to take a practical way of life, but neither could he go along with the Buddhist view of salvation. His standpoint differs from the *nō* writer's or Buddhist's in that Bashō's "poetic spirit" does not deny the values of the present world for the sake of the world yonder. Buddhism would recommend that man should renounce all the worldly values and enter an enlightened realm ruled by the great cosmic law. Bashō, on the other hand, takes an attitude so passive and all-inclusive that he need not renounce anything. For a Buddhist, life exists because there is death. For Bashō, life exists because there is death, indeed; but at the same time death exists because there is life – life is just as important as death. Bashō's ideas on poetry are ultimately the manifestations of such an attitude toward life. *Sabi* and *wabi* are the principles by which man purges his excessive emotions and gains serenity of mind; they enable man to live in this world while transcending it. "Fragrance", "reverberation" and "reflection" are the ideas by which man unites opposites and resolves struggles; they help man to see a correspondence between himself and nature. "Lightness" is a concept through which man recognizes the true value of common ways of living; it teaches man how to endure hardship with a smile, to sympathize with others with a warm heart. Religious pessimism and pragmatic optimism, medieval asceticism and modern humanism, feudalist conservatism and bourgeois liberalism, all are blended in Bashō's poetry. Bashō includes multitudes; he physically lives among them, while detached from them spiritually. "Attain a high stage of en-

---

[64] "Genjū-an no ki", *BI*, 614-615.

lightenment and return to the world of common men" was
his deathbed teaching.[65]

The word *bashō* designates a banana plant, symbolizing the
mutability of life with its large, soft leaves. The poet, in
adopting it for his pseudonym, attempted to overcome sadness
of life by "attaining a high stage of enlightenment" through
*haiku*. Like the water in a shallow sand-bed river, he never
stayed at one place either in actual life or in poetry; he traveled
extensively throughout his life and wrote numerous *haiku* as
he traveled along. Yet *haiku*, after all, was not a religion. As
he grew old, a doubt came upon him as to whether *haiku* itself
was not one of those human passions which kept him from
attaining a higher stage of religious awakening. Day and
night he thought of poetry; as he slept he dreamed of walking
in the morning clouds and in the evening dusk, and as he
awoke he admired the mountains, the water, and wild birds.[66]
He also writes:

No sooner had I decided to give up my poetry and closed my mouth
than a sentiment tempted my heart and something flickered in my
mind. Such is the magic power of the poetic spirit.[67]

Is there a difference between ordinary men's attachment to
material interest and Bashō's to poetry? Bashō tried, as Zeami
did, to bring art and religion together. But gradually he discovered, as Zeami did, that the two could not become one as
long as religion denied some humanistic values which were the
motives of art. Did Bashō finally recognize the priority of
religion to art when, shortly before his death, he referred to
poetry as "sinful attachment"?[68] Whatever the answer may
be, the fact remains that his great poetry is a combined product of the two: his philosophy of life comparable to religion
in its profound understanding of reality, and his art which gave
it a full expression.

[65]  *Sanzōshi, SH*, 162.
[66]  *Oi nikki, Shōmon haikai go-shū*, 13.
[67]  "Seikyo no ben", *BI*, 638.
[68]  *Oi nikki, Shōmon haikai go-shū*, 13.

# CHAPTER III

# W. B. YEATS: IMAGINATION, SYMBOL, AND THE MINGLING OF CONTRARIES

To move from Zeami and Bashō to W. B. Yeats[1] is to jump over a wide gap of time, space, and culture. Numerous points of difference which lie between the Orient and the Occident, between the medieval and the modern age, or between Buddhism and Christianity, separate the Irish poet from the Japanese writers. There is the difference of personality, too: the one was a man of vigorous mind who believed in action, who actively participated in the movement toward his country's independence, whereas the other two were men of delicate temperament who had no interest in politics. Nevertheless, these three writers seem to come very close in some respects. For one thing, they were all artists who conceived art to be a means of perceiving ultimate reality in life. "You are face to face with the heterogeneous", says Yeats in a letter to a friend, "and the test of one's harmony is our power to absorb it and make it harmonious. Gradually these bars, hotels and cottages and strange faces will become familiar, gradually you will come to see them through a mist of half-humorous, half-comical, half-poetical, half-affectionate memories and hopes."[2] Zeami or Bashō would have said this, we are tempted to say, for what they were building up through the nō or haiku was a harmonious vision of the world, too. They were all striving

---

[1] William Butler Yeats (1865-1939) is a well-known Irish poet and playwright. His ideas on poetry are eloquently expressed in his essays and letters, especially in those collected in *Essays* (1924), *Essays, 1931-1936* (1937) and *Letters* (ed. Allan Wade, 1955).
[2] Letter to George Russel, 1898. *Letters*, 294.

for, as Yeats puts it, "a coherent grasping of reality".[3] In the course of doing so they had to face a series of questions that constitute the mysteries of life. "Whether we will or no", says Yeats, "we have to ask ancient questions: Is there reality anywhere? Is there a god? Is there a soul?"[4] Zeami, Bashō, and now Yeats, all asked the questions.

However, while Zeami and Bashō had Buddhism at the basis of their approach toward these issues, Yeats had no conventional religion. Christianity was disappointingly ineffective: "Dissatisfaction with the old idea of God", says Yeats, "cannot but overthrow our sense of order".[5] The mischief started at the end of the seventeenth century "when man became passive before a mechanized nature".[6] Yeats, living in the modern age, looks back to the middle ages with romantic nostalgia:

There, all was an energy flowing outward from the nature itself; here, all is the anxious study and slight deflection of eternal force; there man's mind and body were predominantly subjective; here all is objective, using those words not as philosophy uses them, but as we use them in conversation.[7]

Objective mind, he thinks, continually mistakes a philosophical idea for a spiritual experience. Personal impressions are always checked and finally destroyed by intellectual generalization, by public morality, or by the opinions of the masses. "Life", Yeats believes, "is never the same twice and so cannot be generalised."[8] When life is forced into generalization, it loses its vitality and retains nothing but soulless abstractions. Mathematics, the purest form of abstractions, would maintain that two and two are four, but in actual life no two things are ever alike. People have forgotten that "man has made mathematics, but God reality".[9] They have substituted science for

[3]  Letter to Olivia Shakespear, 1933. *Ibid.*, 806.
[4]  "Modern Poetry", *Essays, 1931-1936*, 21.
[5]  *Pages from a Diary*, 24.
[6]  "Introduction", *The Oxford Book of Modern Verse*, xxvii.
[7]  "The Trembling of the Veil", *Autobiography*, 175.
[8]  Letter to J. B. Yeats, 1909. *Letters*, 534.
[9]  "Private Thoughts", *On the Boiler*, 26.

God, and consequently have lost sight of reality and even know
no way to approach Him. Civilization sleeps in the masses,
wisdom in science; men are entirely astray.

> Turning and turning in the widening gyre
> The falcon cannot hear the falconer;
> Things fall apart; the centre cannot hold;
> Mere anarchy is loosed upon the world, ....[10]

There are intellectual agreements, propagandas, or dogmas.
But emotional agreements, which are so much more lasting
and put no constraint upon the soul, are all gone.[11] Yeats rejected science throughout his life. As a little boy he hated it
with "monkish hate"; several weeks before his death he wrote:
"The abstract is not life and everywhere draws out its contradictions."[12] Man can embody truth, but he cannot know it.
Modern man, misled by science, believes that he can know
truth.

Poetry, which aims at the embodiment of truth, should
therefore expel from itself all abstractions and mechanisms.
Victorian literature, however, was filled with them – scientific
humanitarian preoccupation, psychological curiosity, rhetoric,
utilitarianism. Tennyson's poetry is permeated with scientific
and moral discursiveness: "When he should have been broken-
hearted," Yeats was fond of quoting Verlaine's remark on
*In Memoriam*, "he had many reminiscences".[13] Browning's
verse lacks power as it devotes itself to the analysis of psychology; he had to overuse exclamations and unnatural word-
order in order to give his poetry a forceful appearance. Swinburne, Macaulay and Kipling were merely political rhetori-
cians; their writings are "the soulless self-reflections of man's
skill", as Rossetti called them.[14] George Eliot, always concerned with philosophy and ethics, could not think of any

[10]   "The Second Coming", *Collected Poems*, 184.
[11]   "If I were Four-and-Twenty", *If I were Four-and-Twenty*, 5.
[12]   Letter to Lady Elizabeth Pelham, 1939. *Letters*, 922.
[13]   "Introduction", *The Oxford Book of Modern Verse*, ix.
[14]   *Ibid.*, xviii.

literature as important unless it served the state.[15]  Yeats sums up the trend:

In the Victorian era the most famous poetry was often a passage in a poem of some length, perhaps of great length, a poem full of thoughts that might have been expressed in prose. A short lyric seemed an accident, an interruption amid more serious work ... Swinburne, Tennyson, Arnold, Browning had admitted so much psychology, science, moral fervour.[16]

Victorian poetry has been buried under fragmentary sensuous beauty or detachable ideas – "the impurities". Their evil is that it has deprived a poet of the power to mould vast material into a single image, to create harmony out of chaos. The main target of young anti-Victorian writers was these "impurities" of poetry. The Pre-Raphaelite, Art for Art's Sake, and Rhymer's Club movements were all reactions against Victorian poetry.

So they all defied science, abstraction, morality, rhetoric, psychology; but after the rejection something had to be set up, a scheme which would unify the fragments left in the ruins. Yeats naturally turned to the opposites of these – imagination, emotion, mysticism, magic, symbolism. As a youth he was a fervent admirer of Blake and Shelley, who he thought were champions of imagination in the age of reason. "The world of imagination is infinite and eternal", he quoted from Blake with enthusiasm, "whereas the world of generation or vegetation is finite and temporal. There exist in that eternal world the eternal realities of everything which we see reflected in the vegetable glass of nature."[17]  While intellect separates us from fresh and immediate experience, emotion enlarges, enriches and deepens our experience. Reason, which is deduction from the observation of the senses, binds us to mortality because it binds us to the senses; it divides us from each other by showing us our clashing interests. "But", Yeats says, "imagination divides us from mortality by the immortality of beauty, and

[15]  "At Stratford-on-Avon", *Essays*, 125.
[16]  "Modern Poetry", *Essays, 1931-1936*, 11.
[17]  "Symbolism in Painting", *Essays*, 186.

binds us to each other by opening the secret doors of all hearts".[18] Everything that lives is holy; passions are most holy because they are most living. In fact, our imaginations are but fragments of the universal imagination, portions of the universal body of God. Therefore, as we enlarge our imagination by imaginative sympathy and transform with the beauty and peace of art the sorrows and joys of the world, we put off the limited mortal man more and more and put on the unlimited "immortal man".[19] An artist, pursuing the universal imagination, discovers immortal moods in mortal desires, an undecaying hope in our trivial ambitions, a divine love in sexual passion.[20]

Yeats's belief that imagination can lead us beyond the limitation of the senses is based on his own theory of the human mind. The theory centers upon three doctrines:

(1) That the border of our mind are ever shifting, and that many minds can flow into one another, as it were, and create or reveal a single mind, a single energy.

(2) That the borders of our memories are as shifting, and that our memories are a part of one great memory, the memory of Nature itself.

(3) That this great mind and great memory can be evoked by symbols.[21]

Elsewhere Yeats remarks: "All was indeed but one life flowing everywhere, and taking one quality here, another there."[22] The energy that fills nature flows in men, too. The mental outlooks of men may differ one from another, but they are equally manifestations of one single energy. The energy is not stagnant but flowing; it may at times show conflicts, but will ultimately flow into one stream. Behind the momentary self, which acts and lives in the world and is subject to the

[18] "William Blake and the Imagination", *Essays*, 138.
[19] "William Blake and his Illustrations to *The Divine Comedy*", *Essays*, 170-171.
[20] "The Moods", *Essays*, 240.
[21] "Magic", *Essays*, 33.
[22] "Thoughts on Lady Gregory's Translations", *The Cutting of an Agate*, 26.

judgement of the world, there is that which cannot be called before any mortal judgement seat.[23] The buried self is immortal, because it is at one with the energy of the universe that eternally flows. "I know now", says Yeats, "that revelation is from the self, but from that agelong memoried self, that shapes the elaborate shell of the mollusc and the child in the womb, that teaches the birds to make their nests, and that genius is a crisis that joins that buried self for certain moments to our trivial daily mind."[24] Revelation may be brought forth by the conscious effort of a genius, a magician or a theosophist. But it may occur at random when "the deeps are loosened", taking the form of a miracle. Miracles are a form of revelation and extremely important; historians should remember angels and devils not less than kings and soldiers, plotters and thinkers.[25]

Since the borders of our mind can flow into one another, our individual memories can blend into one another and form the Great Memory, the memory of nature. External incidents happen, cease, and never return; but they leave impressions upon our mind, which we keep as memories. We accumulate memories and go back to them again and again while we live; when we die we hand them down to our next generation. Sometimes before our mind's eye there come images which we are to discover presently in some books we have never read; we have no way to explain this phenomenon except by assuming the Great Memory which passes from generation to generation.[26] The Great Memory is what gives vitality to men's thoughts age after age; it is what renews the world; our individual thoughts are not the deep but little foams upon the deep. Imagination always seeks to remake the world according to the impulses and patterns of the Great Memory. It is as if each man were passing through a stream of suggestions, all streams acting and reacting upon one another no

[23] "At Stratford-on-Avon", *Essays*, 125.
[24] "The Trembling of the Veil", *Autobiography*, 164.
[25] "Magic", *Essays*, 49.
[26] "Anima Mundi", *Essays*, 510.

matter how distant the minds, how dumb the lips. Or, to use another of Yeats's metaphors, a man walked, as it were, casting a shadow, and yet one could never say which was man and which was shadow, or how many the shadows that he cast.[27] A shadow may disappear as the man dies, but his son, his grandson, his friends continue casting their shadows, keeping alive the hidden world of shadows. In fact, all that we do with intensity has an origin in this hidden world and is the symbol or expression of its powers.[28]

Yeats tried to give public sanction to his theory of human mind, first by tying it with Irish mythology and later by developing it into a new, elaborate myth. His lifelong interest in Irish folklore and mythology stems from his belief in the collective memory of a race, in what he calls "the nation-wide multiform reverie".[29] He liked the ancient story-tellers of Ireland because they were more anxious to describe energetic characters and to invent beautiful stories than to express themselves with perfect dramatic logic or in perfectly ordered words. Stories and characters were the common property of the whole race; even when some story-teller added a new incident to a story he never thought of claiming for himself what so obviously lived its own merry or mournful life.[30] Those story-tellers believed in the historical reality of even their wildest imaginings. This is true not in Ireland alone but in any other country: Yeats is fascinated, for the same reason, with the stories of a country as remote as fourteenth-century Japan. "I love", he explains, "all the arts that can still remind me of their origin among the common people, and my ears are only comfortable when the singer sings as if mere speech had taken fire, when he appears to have passed into song almost imperceptibly."[31] This, incidentally, was Yeats's apo-

[27] "The Trembling of the Veil", *Autobiography*, 158.
[28] Letter to Florence Farr, 1901. Quoted in Ellmann, *Yeats: The Man and the Masks*, 113.
[29] "The Trembling of the Veil", *Autobiography*, 158.
[30] "Thoughts on Lady Gregory's Translations", *The Cutting of An Agate*, 2-3.
[31] "Certain Noble Plays of Japan", *Essays*, 275.

logy for including Japanese *nō* plays in the Cuala Press Irish Literature Series. Certainly Yeats must have longed for a country like Zeami's Japan, a country "where all classes share in a half-mythological, half-philosophical folk-belief which the writer and his small audience lift into a new subtlety".[32] Yeats's picture of ideal Ireland exemplifies the same view:

And then Ireland too, as we think, will be a country where not only will the wealth be well distributed but where there will be an imaginative culture and power to understand imaginative and spiritual things distributed among the people. We wish to preserve an ancient ideal of life. Wherever its customs prevail, there you will find the folk song, the folk tale, the proverb and the charming manners that come from ancient culture.[33]

Yet Ireland did not quite become the country Yeats hoped it would. He therefore had to look somewhere else to find a system that would endorse his theory. He found it; or rather, he founded it himself since he could not find it in the existing tradition. His well-known and much debated system, expounded in *A Vision*, should be taken as his private machinery to give a definite pattern to his private views. "I have often had the fancy", he says at the age of thirty-six, "that there is some one myth for every man, which, if we but know it, would make us understand all he did and thought."[34] So Yeats created his own myth. "I have constructed a myth", he says at sixty-six, referring to *A Vision*, "but then one can believe in a myth – one only assents to philosophy."[35] Just as Christian metaphysics would mean nothing to those who do not believe in Christ, Yeats's system would seem nonsense to those who do not believe in it. One is often tempted to compare, for example, his theory of primary and antithetical cones with modern psychologists' ideas on subjectivity and objectivity in human personality. It would be inappropriate, however, to test the

[32] "Note on 'The Only Jealousy of Emer'", *Plays and Controversies*, 434.
[33] A speech in New York, 1904. Quoted in Ellmann, *Yeats: The Man and the Masks*, 113.
[34] "At Stratford-on-Avon", *Essays*, 131.
[35] Letter to Olivia Shakespear, 1931. *Letters*, 781.

validity of a private, subjective system by the standard of a public, objective system. Yeats's idea of the cones, the Phases of the Moon, and the Great Year, for instance, invites emotional sanction rather than logical proof. We should take it for granted that to accept someone's personal system of metaphysics is very difficult; we live in a mythless society, and even the established religions are falling apart – or have fallen apart. The value of a myth does not depend on the number of people who accept it. If we take interest in someone's myth at all and wish to investigate its value, we should at least tentatively accept the system and see how it works as a whole. With a scientific theory we may accept only some parts of it and still make use of them, but with a myth we cannot believe in parts; we must believe in its whole. Its value is determined by what we gain from the belief. Unfortunately Yeats's system is a very elaborate one and needs a great deal of sustained thinking; this often makes one wonder whether one will get enough compensation for all one's effort to follow it through.

A system of metaphysics requires a person to believe in its whole structure before it can be of any value to him. A poem, on the other hand, makes no such demand. Yeats himself seems to admit the natural tendency of a person to believe in immediate life-experience more readily than in the metaphysics of an established religion, for he says: "When I close my eyes and pronounce the word 'Christianity' and wait for its unconscious suggestion, I do not see Christ crucified, or the Good Shepherd from the catacombs, but a father and mother and their children, a picture by Leonardo da Vinci most often..."[36] His view on the relationship among literature, religion and philosophy is more explicit in the following passage:

In Christianity what was philosophy in Eastern Asia became life, biography and drama. A play passes through the same process in being written. At first, if it has psychological depth, there is a bundle of ideas, something that can be stated in philosophical terms; my *Countess Cathleen*, for instance, was once the moral ques-

[36] "If I were Four-and-Twenty", *If I were Four-and-Twenty*, 12.

tion, may a soul sacrifice itself for a good end? but gradually philosophy is eliminated until at last the only philosophy audible, if there is even that, is the mere expression of one character or another. When it is completely life it seems to the hasty reader a mere story.[37]

Religion, a system of metaphysics, is closer to immediate life-experience than philosophy, a system of abstractions; yet one must still believe in the system in order to absorb the wisdom of religion. But drama does not have to refer to something outside in the manner in which a religious teaching falls back on the central principles of that religion. A play creates its own world; it creates its own law within the vision it presents. Yeats makes a similar comment on poetry, too: "A poem should be a law to itself as plants and beasts are."[38]

A work of literature, then, expresses hidden eternal truth, the treasure of the Great Memory, just as folk literature or religion does. But a work of art, unlike the other two, does not or need not rely on mythology or metaphysics to make itself emotionally convincing. The weapon of art, as Yeats thinks, is symbolism. We have already noted that in the third doctrine of the great mind he says: "This great mind and great memory can be evoked by symbols." "A symbol", he reiterates elsewhere, "is indeed the only possible expression of some invisible essence, a transparent lamp about a spiritual flame."[39] Therefore a poet, whose duty is to express invisible essence, must look for a symbol or create one. Yeats writes:

It is only by ancient symbols, by symbols that have numberless meanings beside the one or two the writer lays an emphasis upon, or the half-score he knows of, that any highly subjective art can escape from the barrenness and shallowness of a too conscious arrangement, into the abundance and depth of nature. The poet of essences and pure ideas must seek in the half-lights that glimmer from symbol to symbol as if to the ends of the earth, all that the epic and dramatic poet finds of mystery and shadow in the accidental circumstances of life.[40]

[37]  "Estrangement", *Autobiography*, 284.
[38]  Letter to Katharine Tynan, 1888. *Letters*, 86.
[39]  "William Blake and his Illustrations to *The Divine Comedy*", *Essays*, 142.
[40]  "The Philosophy of Shelley's Poetry", *Essays*, 107.

Yeats is talking about what we may call the traditional symbol. The power of the symbol lies in its multiplicity of meaning acquired by its evolution through history. It expands in meaning because it suggests rather than states, because it works instantaneously and imaginatively upon our mind and brings us a number of historical and personal associations. It transcends the limitation of time and place; it leads us into the abundance and depth of eternal nature.

Yet there is another kind of symbol, what Yeats calls the arbitrary symbol. The concept is a corollary from his idea of personal myth: as there is a myth for each person, there should be a personal symbol or symbols for each man. Individual men are different; each has his own approach to ultimate reality; one man's symbol, consequently, cannot be exactly identical with that of someone else. "In the second part of Oisin", writes Yeats, "under disguise of symbolism I have said several things to which I only have the key. The romance is for my readers. They must not even know there is a symbol anywhere."[41] This statement, made when the poet was only twenty-four, pushes the point a little too far. The later poetry of Yeats contains many personal or semi-personal symbols – a swan, a unicorn, a tower; yet they are explicitly defined by their respective contexts.

However, the distinction between these two types of symbols came to mean little. Yeats explains:

At first I tried to distinguish between symbols and symbols, between what I called inherent symbols and arbitrary symbols, but the distinction has come to mean little or nothing. Whether their power has arisen out of themselves, or whether it has an arbitrary origin, matters little, for they act, as I believe, because the great memory associates them with certain events and moods and persons. Whatever the passions of man have gathered about, becomes a symbol in the great memory, and in the hands of him who has the secret, it is a worker of wonders, a caller-up of angels or of devils. The symbols are of all kinds, for everything in heaven or earth has its association, momentous or trivial, in the great mem-

[41]  Letter to Katharine Tynan, 1888. *Letters*, 88.

ory, and never knows what forgotten events may have plunged it,
like toadstool and the ragweed, into the great passions.[42]

✓The traditional symbol and the personal symbol, although
they may differ in origin, are really one. ✓The personal symbol
is created by a poet in a trance, when his memories are united
with the Great Memory. His imagination moves "in a dim
world like the country of sleep in *Love's Nocturne* and 'Siren
there winds her dizzy hair sings'." If he is to sojourn there a
while, that world will grow consistent with itself, and emotion
will be related to emotion by a system of ordered images as in
*The Divine Comedy*.[43] The images in such a state are impersonal
in the sense that they are separate from the poet's ordinary
self; they have their independent lives. Yeats explains this
with examples:

⌐ Michael Angelo's 'Moses', Velasquez' 'Philip the Second', the
colour purple, a crucifix, call into life an emotion or state that vanishes with them because they are its only possible expression, and
that is why no mind is more valuable than the images it contains.
The imaginative writer differs from the saint in that he identifies
himself – to the neglect of his own soul, alas! – with the soul of the
world, and frees himself from all that is impertinent in that soul...[44]

/ A poet would neglect his mind for the sake of the images it
contains; he would leave his personal soul in order to join
the impersonal soul. His images, if they are lasting ones, will
become symbols in the storehouse of the Great Memory.
✓ It is in this connection that Yeats insists on the idea of
impersonal poetry. He thinks that a poet should apply himself to a form of meditation which permits an image or symbol
to generate itself. The images and symbols thus generated
will then gradually "build themselves up into coherent struc-
tures often beautiful and startling".[45] Not every poet can do
this. It is the privilege of a poet who, either by natural gift
or by training, is able to pass into a slight trance. When the

[42]   "Magic", *Essays*, 60-61.
[43]   "Discoveries", *Essays*, 363.
[44]   *Ibid.*, 354.
[45]   "Prometheus Unbound", *Essays, 1931-1936*, 58.

poet in such a state suspends the intellect and critical faculty, he will see images passing before him. When he suspends also desire and lets them form at their own desire, the images will become more clear in color and more precise in articulation, both he and the images moving in the midst of a powerful light. The images are from the "subconscious"; his mind has become a polished mirror which reflects them. Yeats sums it up:

Does not all art come when a nature, that never ceases to judge itself, exhausts personal emotion in action or desire so completely that something impersonal, something that has nothing to do with action or desire, suddenly starts into its place, something which is as unforeseen, as completely organized, even as unique, as the images that pass before the mind between sleeping and waking?[46]

In the same vein he comments: "A good scenario writes itself, it puts words into the mouths of all its characters while we sleep, but a bad scenario exacts the most miserable toil."[47] Here Yeats comes close to the idea of inspiration. In fact he asks the question: "When a man writes any work of genius, or invents some creative action, is it not because some knowledge or power has come into his mind from beyond his mind?"[48] His own answer, of course, is in the affirmative. His Muse, however, is an image or symbol which, springing out of the unconscious, works upon the poet's mind with a magical power. An ideal poet would live, therefore, "but for the moment when vision comes to [his] weariness like terrible lightning".[49]

The idea of impersonality in artistic creation is closely related to Yeats's famous theory of the "anti-self" or the mask. Yeats, recalling his young days of apprenticeship in verse-writing, says that he always tried to put his very self into poetry, that he understood this as a representation of his own visions and an attempt to cut away the non-essential, but that

[46]  "Anima Mundi", *Essays*, 508-509.
[47]  "The Trembling of the Veil", *Autobiography*, 200.
[48]  Letter to Sean O'Casey, 1928. *Letters*, 741-742.
[49]  "The Trembling of the Veil", *Autobiography*, 164.

when he imagined the visions outside of himself his imagination became full of decorative landscape and of still life. Then
a revelation came upon him:

> Then one day I understood quite suddenly, as the way is, that I
> was seeking something unchanging and unmixed and always out-
> side myself, a Stone or an Elixir that was always out of reach, and
> that I myself was the fleeting thing that held out its hand. The
> more I tried to make my art deliberately beautiful, the more did I
> follow the opposite of myself, for deliberate beauty is like a woman
> always desiring man's desire.[50]

Yeats's mask has multiple meanings: the social self in contrast
to the private, the self in other people's consciousness in contrast to the self conceived by itself, and so forth. But its most
important meaning pertaining to poetry seems to be suggested
in the passage just quoted. The poet's ego, the self known to
him, is trivial and mortal; therefore, as long as he tries to
write verse out of this self, he will forever remain on the level of
the sentimental and decorative. If he wants something pure
and unchanging, he must destroy his own ego and create its
"anti-self". Yeats explains elsewhere: "A writer must die
every day he lives, be reborn, as it is said in the Burial Service,
an incorruptible self, that self opposite of all that he has named
'himself'."[51] The energy of all creative and joyous life is a
rebirth as something not oneself. If we cannot imagine ourselves as different from what we are and assume the second
self, how can we impose a discipline upon ourselves? how can
we escape from the passive acceptance of the current moral
code?[52] To wear a mask, therefore, is the condition of arduous
full life. Yet, the more intense and profound the man's concept of the mask is, the more difficult it will be for him to attain the mask. The mask, as Yeats defines it, is an emotional
antithesis to all that comes out of man's internal nature.[53] The
deeper he digs into his internal nature, the more obstacles he

[50]    "Anima Hominis", *Essays*, 503.
[51]    "Discoveries", *Essays*, 336.
[52]    "Dramatis Personae", *Autobiography*, 277.
[53]    "Estrangement", *Autobiography*, 285.

will build between himself and his anti-self. Any sincere poet always suffers this dilemma. "The poet", says Yeats, "finds and makes his mask in disappointment, the hero in defeat. The desire that is satisfied is not a great desire, nor has the shoulder used all its might that an unbreakable gate has never strained."[54] All intense life is tragic. We begin to live when we have conceived life as tragedy.

Yet, as Yeats thinks, modern men have lost the sense of tragic life. As time has progressed, men's life has grown safer; the sense of comedy has become their social bond. Even some of the greatest modern writers – Shelley, Ruskin, Wordsworth – are in their belief descendants of Rousseau; they always dwell upon good only, making a clear contrast with Shakespeare, Villon, Dante and Cervantes who drew their strength and weight from their preoccupation with evil.[55] In the modern age human nature has lost its antagonist; men have lost aspiration, energy and joy. What they think is tragedy is really a work of passive suffering – *Empedocles on Etna*, for example. True tragedy, in Yeats's opinion, lies in pure passion, in most intense passion. It tries to exclude or lessen "character", to diminish the power of daily mood, to cheat or blind its too clear perception. For Yeats "character" and "personality" denote two different things: "character" means the public self, the conscious part of personality which faces and observes the outside world; "personality"is the private self, the sum total of passions and desires which differs from person to person.[56] True tragedy, as Yeats thinks, depicts a private world where "personality" reigns. "If the real world is not altogether rejected", he says, "it is but touched here and there, and into the places we have left empty we summon rhythm, balance, pattern, images that remind us of vast passions, the vagueness of past times, all the chimeras that haunt the edge of trance."[57] True tragedy is poetic, and true poetry tragic.

[54]   "The Trembling of the Veil", *Autobiography*, 116.
[55]   "Anima Hominis", *Essays*, 500.
[56]   "If I were Four-and-Twenty", *If I were Four-and-Twenty*, 15.
[57]   "The Tragic Theatre", *Essays*, 300-301.

According to Yeats, the traditionally held antithesis between "character" and lyric poetry in dramatic literature is a product of the modern age. If we go back a few centuries and enter the great periods of drama in Greece, France and England, "character" grows less and sometimes disappears, while a good deal of lyric feeling emerges and often a lyric measure is worked into the dialogue. Then we discover that in the works of great dramatists – in Corneille, in Racine, in Greek playwrights – there is no "character", since its place is taken by passions and motives, one person being jealous, another full of love or remorse or pride or anger.[58] In these great tragedies the persons on the stage grow greater and greater till they are humanity itself. "We feel our minds expand convulsively", Yeats writes, "or spread out slowly like some moon-brightened image-crowded sea. That which is before our eyes perpetually vanishes and returns again in the midst of the excitement it creates, and the more enthralling it is, the more do we forget it."[59] Seeing the play acted, we, the audience, are allured almost to the intensity of trance. To describe the feeling even the word joy is not enough, because it is really not joy as we understand the term. It is ecstasy, which arises from the contemplation of things vaster than the individual and imperfectly seen, perhaps, by all those that still live. "Is not ecstasy some fulfilment of the soul in itself", Yeats asks, "some slow or sudden expansion of it like an overflowing well? Is not this what is meant by beauty?"[60]

The aim of poetry, or of tragedy, is the creation of such a feeling – ecstasy, "pure, aimless joy", in which a person's soul is united with the great soul. Tragedy, as Yeats thinks, is a literary form in which a certain great character is led to his final glory. If farce is the struggle against a ridiculous object and comedy against a movable object, tragedy is the desperate fight against an immovable object; tragedy, therefore, is the most noble. When the hero's despair steadily mounts and

[58] *Ibid.*, 296-297.
[59] *Ibid.*, 303.
[60] "Estrangement", *Autobiography*, 286.

finally reaches its limit, it will become a pure, aimless joy, though the man, the shade, may still mourn his lost object; his personal sorrow transforms itself into eternal delight.[61] "In all the great tragedies", says Yeats, "tragedy is a joy to the man who dies; in Greece the tragic chorus danced."[62] In order to achieve this kind of ecstasy, literature needs three things which Kant thought we must postulate to make life livable – Freedom, God, and Immortality. Freedom provides us with courage and dignity; when it is gone we have Stendhal's "mirror dawdling down a lane". God gives us an object for our aspiration or struggle; when He is gone we have realism and the accidental. Immortality turns our notion of death from the fearful to the joyous; when it is gone we can no longer write a tragedy.[63] Here Yeats seems to be approaching the Aristotelian concept of tragedy. With the notion of Freedom and Immortality on one hand, and that of God on the other, man is alternately seized upon by the sense of pride and of insignificance. When the two emotions meet and momentarily keep a perilous balance, there emerges a tragic life. "I am always", says Yeats, "in all I do, driven to a moment which is the realisation of myself as unique and free, or to a moment which is the surrender to God of all that I am ... Could those two impulses, one as much as a part of truth as the other, be reconciled, or if one or the other could prevail, all life would cease."[64] The tragic hero is the most heroic of men, because he is most vital, because he contains in himself widely antithetical emotions and carries them to extremity, until they blend into the condition of fire. Timon of Athens contemplates his own end and orders his tomb, Cleopatra sets the asp to her bosom; their words move us because their sorrow is not their own but is heightened to intensity, has become all men's fate. Such is the function of art:

That shaping joy has kept the sorrow pure, as it had kept it were

---

[61]  "Other Matters", *On the Boiler*, 35.
[62]  "Introduction", *The Oxford Book of Modern Verse*, xxxiv-xxxv.
[63]  *Pages from a Diary*, 49-50.
[64]  *Ibid.*, 19.

the emotion love or hate, for the nobleness of the Arts is in the mingling of contraries, the extremity of sorrow, the extremity of joy, perfection of personality, the perfection of its surrender, over-flowing turbulent energy, and marmorean stillness; and its red rose opens at the meeting of the two beams of the cross, and at the trysting place of mortal and immortal, time and eternity.[65]

Yeats's favorite play by Shakespeare was *King Lear*.

Yeats's concept of a great man is a person capable of be-coming a tragic hero, having all human emotions in their greatest intensity. A sage has all-round, harmonious per-sonality; a fool has no personality; yet these two are far away from humanity, they do not exist in actual life. A great man has profound desires, so profound that they cannot be ful-filled. D. H. Lawrence once said that it would be terrible to desire and not possess; yet on the other hand it will also be terrible to possess and not desire.[66] A man is an artifice, an emphasis, an uncompleted arc. "Because the life man sees is not the final end of things", Yeats explains, "the moment we attain to greatness of any kind by personal labour and will we become fragmentary, and find no task in active life which can use our finest faculties. We are compelled to think and express and not to do."[67] Those who deeply think and adequately express are artists; at least those were the artists of ancient times. They always endeavored to create most passionate men. If they had carried their aesthetic theory to its conclu-sion, they would have created one single type of man, one single type of woman, gathering up by a kind of deification a capacity for all energy and all passion, into a Krishna, a Christ, a Dionysus. Even in modern times a poetical painter such as Botticelli or Rossetti, in his supreme achievement, paints one type of face known afterwards by his name.[68] Of Rossetti in particular:

If he painted a flame or a blue distance, he painted as though he had seen the flame out of whose heart all flames had been taken, or

[65]  "Poetry and Patriotism", *Poetry and Ireland*, 12.
[66]  Letter to Olivia Shakespear, 1933. *Letters*, 810.
[67]  "Estrangement", *Autobiography*, 288.
[68]  "The Death of Synge", *ibid.*, 304.

the blue of the abyss that was before all life; and if he painted a woman's face he painted it in some moment of intensity when the ecstasy of the lover and of the saint are alike, and desire becomes wisdom without ceasing to be desire. He listens to the cry of the flesh till it becomes proud and passes beyond the world where some immense desire that the intellect cannot understand mixes with the desire of a body's warmth and softness.[69]

Similarly a poet must live the most intense life, a life that burns, in Pater's phrase, "with the gemlike flame".

Yeats's concept of ideal life is related to his idea of beauty on the one hand, and to that of philosophy on the other. To Yeats, particularly before the turn of the century, beauty meant "the impossible purity" which lies in the woman of all women, in the flame of all flames. It was a sign of eternity. He believed, therefore, that man would arrive at the divine essence by always desiring beauty in all things. While "infected" things are ugly, eternal things are beautiful; beauty is the mark that distinguishes the eternal from the temporal. If we aspire for the beautiful, we shall all be artists, apostles of beauty. Yeats quotes Blake with approval: "Christianity is Art", and "the whole business of man is the arts."[70] Poetry, in particular, should be generated out of the poet's strenuous pursuit of beauty, for its value wholly depends upon the amount of eternity it embodies. "Beauty", Yeats says, "is the end and law of poetry."[71] Poetry endeavors to find beauty in all things, philosophy, nature, passion. In so far as it rejects beauty it destroys its own right to exist.

However, a poet's vigorous pursuit of beauty should not mean that beauty is his sole aim. On the contrary, beauty is the effect rather than the cause, the means rather than the end. Beauty is the end of poetry only in the sense that it is a sign by which the goal is made visible. Where there is profound emotion there is always beauty; where there is beauty, however, there is not always profound emotion. By confusing the two some of the *fin de siècle* artists degraded their art to the

[69] "The Happiest of the Poets", *Essays*, 64-65.
[70] "William Blake and his Illustrations to *The Divine Comedy*", *Essays*, 171.
[71] Letter to George Russell, 1900. *Letters*, 343.

level of sensual indulgence. The rebels against Victorianism,
including the young Yeats, so much detested the popular
moralism of the time that they turned away from all ideas.
√They were right in so far as they rejected stock ideas; but they
did not know that there were two important kinds of philosophy – "profound philosophy" and "private philosophy".
The former will still use logical and critical thinking, but it
covers so wide an area and reaches such great depth that it
will come to face the three ultimate questions of life: God,
Heaven, and Immortality. ∨ Philosophy, still believing in
human reason, may deny them all meaning; actually some of
the greatest works of mankind are such denial. Yet it cannot
deny them without despair, without helpless despair.[72] This
is the source of "profound philosophy"; "I think", Yeats says,
"profound philosophy must come from terror."[73] Such despair often evokes a startling inspiration in a writer and leads
him to the creation of a great literary work. When he creates
a great work, he will find that he has created a myth, "a private philosophy", which strives to overcome the despair. He
has found a way to salvation; he has founded a religion. All
great poets do this. When Yeats and his friends set up the
Hermetic society, he made a proposal:

I had, when we first made our society, proposed for our considera-
tion that whatever the great poets had affirmed in their finest
moments was the nearest we could come to an authoritative religion, and that their mythology, their spirit of water and wind
were but literal truth.[74]

"All our art", he says elsewhere, "is but the putting our faith
and the evidence of our faith into words or forms and our
faith is in ecstasy."[75] "All symbolic art", he says again,
"should arise out of a real belief."[76] This leads him to an
explicit denial of art for art's sake: "Literature must be the
expression of conviction, and be the garment of noble emotion,

[72] "Bishop Berkeley", *Essays, 1931-1936*, 44.
[73] "Modern Poetry", *Essays, 1931-1936*, 21.
[74] "Reveries", *Autobiography*, 55.
[75] Letter to J. B. Yeats, 1913. *Letters*, 583.
[76] "Discoveries", *Essays*, 364.

and not an end in itself."[77] Philosophy is needed, and not needed, in poetry. To sum up the relation Yeats remarks:

> Goethe said the poet needs all philosophy but must keep it out of his work. I am writing a play on the death of Cuchulain, an episode or two from the old epic. My "private philosophy" is there but there must be no sign of it; all must be like an old fairy tale. It guides me to certain conclusions and gives me precision but I do not write it.[78]

A poet should reject "public philosophy", the system of abstract ideas; but he does need "private philosophy", the scheme of interpreting personal experience. Nevertheless the writer must not write it, because a literary work presents a self-contained vision, a microcosm which has no room for anything that does not belong to it. To borrow Yeats's metaphor, a work of art is a fire that must burn up everything but itself; the whole history of the world must be reduced to wallpaper before which the *dramatis personae* must pose and speak.[79]

Understanding what Yeats thinks is the aim of poetry, we are not at all surprized to know that he insists on the oneness of all arts. If an ideal painter is the one who represents the divine essence through symbolism, a perfect poet is the one who does the same; thus Yeats praises the poetry of Blake and Shelley in the same terms as he does Rossetti's painting. In ancient times all arts were one, since people had an ideal of life common to all. When this ideal is rediscovered, music and poetry, painting and literature, will again draw closer together.[80] They will all move, of course, from the abstract and utilitarian, and advance toward the immediate, individual, sensuous and symbolic. They will move in the direction of music, because music is the most subjective and sensuous of all arts. Yeats agrees with Pater in believing that all arts would approach, if

---

[77]  "Hopes and Fears for Irish Literature", *United Ireland*, XII (Oct. 15, 1892), 5. Quoted in Ellmann, *Yeats: The Man and the Masks*, 142.
[78]  Letter to Ethel Mannin, 1938. *Letters*, 917-918.
[79]  Letter to Sean O'Casey, 1928. *Letters*, 741.
[80]  "Estrangement", *Autobiography*, 298.

they were able, close to "the condition of music".[81] While confessing that he was tone-deaf, Yeats was most respectful of music throughout his life. He spoke verses in a kind of chant when he was making them; sometimes, when he was alone on a country road, he would speak them in a loud chanting voice; he felt he would speak them in that way to other people if he dared.[82]

It is also for this reason that Yeats emphasizes the importance of rhythm in verse. While a sentence constructed by pure logic is abstract and lifeless, rhythm implies "a living body, a breast to rise and fall, or limbs that dance".[83] A good artist arranges his subject not consciously and deliberately but subconsciously and intuitively; he does this through rhythm. Rhythm is the voice of the subconscious; it leads us into that state of real trance in which we are both asleep and awake, in which our mind is liberated from the pressure of the will.[84] Rhythm, therefore, is what separates good writing from bad; it is "the glimmer, the fragrance, the spirit of all literature".[85] In our verse-writing we should make most of rhythm, a rhythm such as would best invoke the subconscious:

> ... we would seek out those wavering, meditative, organic rhythms, which are the embodiment of the imagination, that neither denies nor hates, because it has done with time, and only wishes to gaze upon some reality, some beauty ... The form of sincere poetry, unlike the form of the popular poetry, may indeed be sometimes obscure, or ungrammatical as in some of the best of the Songs of Innocence and Experience...[86]

The poet deals with something that moves beyond our senses. He will not be able to express it successfully unless his words are "as subtle, as complex, as full of mysterious life, as the body of a flower or of a woman".

---

[81]   "Note on the First Performance of 'At the Hawk's Well'", *Plays and Controversies*, 418-419.
[82]   "Speaking to the Psaltery", *Essays*, 17-18.
[83]   Letter to J. B. Yeats, 1916. *Letters*, 608.
[84]   "The Symbolism of Poetry", *Essays*, 195-196.
[85]   "Speaking to the Psaltery", *Essays*, 22.
[86]   "The Symbolism of Poetry", *Essays*, 201-202.

In an attempt to bring words and music together, Yeats wrote a number of poems for music in his later years; one collection is even called *Words for Music Perhaps*. But his ambition to unite all arts is best seen in his playwriting. As early as in 1905 he expressed his admiration of Synge's drama in which "word and phrase dance to a very strange rhythm".[87] When he came to participate in the new Irish theater movement, he expounded his idea of poetic drama more positively and vehemently. He said:

> We must get rid of everything that is restless, everything that draws attention away from the sound of voice, or from the few moments of intense expression, whether that expression is through the voice or through the hands; we must from time to time substitute for the moments that the eyes see the nobler moments that the heart sees, the rhythmical movements that seem to flow up into the imagination from some deeper life than that of the individual soul.[88]

Yeats proposed to simplify, not only gesture and speech but also scenery and costume on the stage. "They should be little more than an unobstrusive pattern", he said. "There must be nothing unnecessary, nothing that will distract the attention from speech and movement."[89] All of Yeats's plays are along this line. His most elaborate, if not successful, effort toward the amalgamation of all arts came when he wrote *Four Plays for Dancers*. Largely inspired by the Japanese *nō* drama, these plays were written in an attempt to create "a different form of art". In *At the Hawk's Well*, for instance, there is no stage property except a patterned screen. There are three musicians, with a drum, a gong, and a zither; they play a music which is so simple that "anyone with a fair idea of music could learn in a few days".[90] The movements of the players are highly stylized; they must move "a little stiffly and gravely like marionettes" and to the accompaniment of drum taps.

[87]  "Preface to the First Edition of the *Well of the Saints*", *Essays*, 371.
[88]  "Irish Dramatic Movement", *Collected Works*, IV, 115.
[89]  *Ibid.*, 115.
[90]  Edmund Dulac, "Music for 'At the Hawk's Well'", *Plays and Controversies*, 420.

The words, written of course in verse, are sometimes sung, sometimes half-sung, and sometimes spoken. Of the four persons in the drama two main actors are masked; the faces of the other two are made up to resemble masks. "The face of the speaker", says Yeats, "should be as much a work of art as the lines that he speaks or the costume that he wears."[91] The play begins and ends with the folding and unfolding of a black cloth on which appears a gold pattern suggesting a hawk; one character in the play wears a dress which also suggests a hawk. In view of all this we may say that *Four Plays for Dancers* aim at the unification of poetry, music, singing, dancing, sculpture and painting, all pointing toward the direction of the "distinguished, indirect and symbolic". Apart from the question of theatrical success, these plays seem to represent a phase of Yeats's aesthetics in its most extreme form.

On the whole, Yeats's concept of a poet and poetry was a most lofty one. "A poet", he said, "is by the very nature of things a man who lives with entire sincerity, or rather, the better his poetry the more sincere his life".[92] And sincere life meant to him a life which is always vigorously in pursuit of truth – not abstract truth, but "kind of vision of reality which satisfies the whole being".[93] "I thought", he says, "that if a powerful and benevolent spirit has shaped the destiny of this world, we can better discover that destiny from the words that have gathered up the heart's desire of the world, than from historical records, or from speculation, wherein the heart withers."[94] But the traditional means to discover truth had been destroyed before his time; modern science had done the damage. Yeats had to grope for something that would provide a foundation for his tower among the old ruins – some means of moulding chaos into a coherent pattern. Restlessly he went from one to another – Pre-Raphaelitism, the Rhymer's Club,

[91]  "Preface to the *Four Plays for Dancers*", *Plays and Controversies*, 332.
[92]  Unpublished notes for a London lecture on "Contemporary Poetry", dictated in Dublin in 1910. Quoted in Ellmann, *Yeats: The Man and the Masks*, 5.
[93]  Letter to J. B. Yeats, 1914. *Letters*, 588.
[94]  "The Philosophy of Shelley's Poetry", *Essays*, 79.

theosophy, folk literature, magic, the Great Wheel, the Upa-
nishads. Yet his basic belief never greatly changed: it was a
belief in imagination as against intellect, in the principle of
integrity and assimilation as against that of analysis and dissolution. While emphasizing the individuality of personal
experience, he also tried to see the interrelatedness of all men
in their subconscious selves; he conceived the Great Memory,
rich and eternal, as unifying all human imaginations. Images
and symbols, as he saw them, are the medium through which
man momentarily glances at the ancient memory of his race.
A poet is the person who manipulates these images and symbols, thereby gathering up the heart's desire of the world. He
will try to proceed toward the great desire, the antithesis of
what man in his conscious moments thinks he is. Man's most
profound energy comes out of a life tragically lived. Such will
be the life of a true poet, and his poetry also. When he attains
such an ultimate stage of human life, he will feel neither joy
nor sorrow; he will only feel "ecstasy", an emotion so heightened in intensity that it will burn up all personal elements in
him. The artist, facing eternity, is united with it; he then will,
through his art, receive the eternal source of vitality. This,
and only this, will satisfy all artists' cry:

> Consume my heart away: sick with desire
> And fastened to a dying animal
> It knows not what it is; and gather me
> Into the artifice of eternity.[95]

---

[95] "Sailing to Byzantium", *Collected Poems*, 191.

CHAPTER IV

# EZRA POUND: PRECISION, IMAGE, AND
# IMPERSONAL POETRY


Ezra Pound[1] is beyond doubt one of the most controversial figures in contemporary literature. While he has many followers who consider him as the "creator" of English poetry in our time, he also has a host of enemies who attack him in a language almost as violent as his. This may be attributed to a number of factors. There are his political and economic beliefs, real or misunderstood – anti-Semitism, Fascist sympathy, anti-Americanism, leading up to his recent conviction for treason. There is the question of his personality, allegedly arrogant and dominating; he always wants to teach, or preach, his cause. Another factor is his prose style, which, while it is humorous and has shock-effects, is often boldly unorthodox, bitingly satirical or fiercely militant. But, needless to say, these factors are extraneous to his concept of poetry; they may provide data for evaluating Pound the man, but not his poetry or his aesthetics. Yet still there are other issues which do fall within the realm of poetry: his leadership in the imagist movement and his subsequent departure from it, his association with the vorticist group, his theory and practice of the ideographic method in verse-writing. These issues have been

[1] Ezra Pound (1885- ), an American poet, well-known as the initiator of the so-called Imagist Movement in 1912. His ideas on poetry are set forth in a large number of essays and letters: *The Spirit of Romance* (1910), *Gaudier Brzeska* (1916), *Pavannes and Divisions* (1918), *Instigations* (1920), *Antheil and the Treatise on Harmony* (1924), *Imaginary Letters* (1930), *How to Read* (1931), *The ABC of Reading* (1934), *Make It New* (1934), *Polite Essays* (1937), *Culture* (1939), *Patria Mia* (1950), *The Letters of Ezra Pound* (1950), *Literary Essays of Ezra Pound* (1954), *Pavannes and Divigations* (1958), etc.

controversial because they include certain elements which are radically new, or even revolutionary, to the orthodox poetic tradition. Pound is "eccentric"; his work does not neatly fit into the established patterns of English poetry. Along with T. E. Hulme and T. S. Eliot he is declaredly anti-Romantic, but his imagism, vorticism and ideographic method contain much that is romantic.

However, most of the issues which make Pound a controversial figure will drop off when he is seen on a highly general level of poetics where, for example, Zeami and Bashō also come in. Pound is eccentric and revolutionary, indeed, – but, within the Western poetic tradition. When juxtaposed with Zeami and Bashō, he is unmistakably Western. To treat him in such general terms, of course, will not much reveal the peculiarities of his poetry or poetics. But, when Pound is seen against the background of Western poetic tradition, he is usually criticized and evaluated as a literary innovator, an inventor of new poetic forms – that is, always in historical terms. His essays expounding the imagist or vorticist principles have always been the focus of scholars' attention; his writings on the nature of poetry in general, like an essay called "The Serious Artist", have been largely neglected, since they are regarded simply as a restatement of truisms in Western poetics. But Pound's "revolutionary" ideas are really based on these truisms of Western poetics, as we shall see later in this chapter. The chapter may not much reveal the characteristics of Pound's way of writing poetry, but it will demonstrate, we hope, some basic assumptions of Western poetics on which Pound, even the rebel Pound, seems to stand.

One way to begin a study of Pound's ideas on poetry is through his close friend, W. B. Yeats. Yeats has referred to Pound in several of his prose writings, but one of the most interesting passages appears when he assigns the younger poet to the twenty-third phase of the moon in his system of the Great Wheel. Yeats writes:

I find, at this 23rd Phase which is it is said the first where there is hatred of the abstract, where the intellect turns upon itself, Mr.

Ezra Pound, Mr. Eliot, Mr. Joyce, Signor Pirandello, who either
eliminate from metaphor the poet's phantasy and substitute a
strangeness discovered by historical or contemporary research or
who break up the logical process of thought by flooding them with
associated ideas or words that seem to drift into the mind by
chance.[2]

The two characteristics of the phase, as mentioned here, seem
to suggest the main points at which Yeats and Pound agree
and differ. Yeats certainly hated the abstract, and Pound,
referring to the stagnant state of knowledge in the Middle
Ages, said such things as: "Abstract arguments didn't get
mankind rapidly forward, or rapidly extend the borders of
knowledge."[3] When the two poets lived together in a cottage
on Ashdown Forest in 1913, Pound helped Yeats "to get back
to the definite and concrete, away from modern abstractions",
as the elder poet gratefully acknowledges.[4] But Pound radically differed from Yeats in that he did not try to organize
human experience into any elaborate structure. He had little
interest in intellectual synthesis; he was scornful of all forms of
systematization. As Yeats thought, Pound was primarily a
technician; he perceived all things by touching, tasting and
investigating them technically. Through his technical efficiency he discovered and enjoyed new aspects of the world like
a man who wipes his breath from the window-pane and laughs
in his delight at all the varied scenes that come to his sight.
To Pound life was largely a flux eternally flowing in chaos,
while Yeats considered perfection to lie in a state of harmony
between the flux and conscious limitation.[5] Pound seems to
attribute the origin of his pessimistic world-picture to the
spirit of his age when he says he belonged to a generation which
was unable to work out a code for action. He and his fellow
men believed and disbelieved everything – that is to say, they

[2]   W. B. Yeats, *A Vision* (1925), 211.
[3]   *The ABC of Reading*, 10.
[4]   Joseph Hone, *W. B. Yeats: 1865-1939*, 272.
[5]   For a more extensive treatment of Yeats's criticism of Pound, see H. W.
Häusermann, "W. B. Yeats' Criticism of Ezra Pound", *English Studies*,
XXIX (1948), 97-109.

believed in the individual case. "The best of us", Pound recalls, "accepted every conceivable 'dogma' as a truth for *a* situation, as the truth for a particular crux, crisis or temperament."[6] Pound was a sceptic and relativist.

This relativist concept of truth is the very basis of Pound's views on poetry and the arts. The process from the perception of truth to the formation of poetry is a kind of evolution. Pound summarizes it in a paragraph:

Our only measure of truth is ... our own perception of truth. The undeniable tradition of metamorphosis teaches us that things do not remain always the same. They become other things by swift and unanalysable process. It was only when men began to mistrust the myths and to tell nasty lies about the Gods for a moral purpose that these matters became hopelessly confused. Then some unpleasing Semite or Parsee or Syrian began to use myths for social propaganda, when the myth was degraded into an allegory or a fable, and that was the beginning of the end. And the Gods no longer walked in men's gardens. The first myths arose when a man walked sheer into "nonsense", that is to say, when some very vivid and undeniable adventure befell him, and he told someone else who called him a liar. Thereupon, after bitter experience, perceiving that no one could understand what he meant when he said that he "turned into a tree", he made a myth – a work of art that is – an impersonal or objective story woven out of his own emotion, as the nearest equation that he was capable of putting into words. That story, perhaps, then gave rise to a weaker copy of his emotion in others, until there arose a cult, a company of people who could understand each other's nonsense about the Gods.[7]

Except that Pound perhaps slightly overemphasizes the aspect of communication – or malcommunication – in art, all his basic ideas on poetry are defined or implied here in an organic way. There is no such thing as objective truth, or if there is, man cannot know it becuse he is dependent on the senses which are limited and subjective, and because the level of reality which the senses perceive is always changing. People of old recognized this fact, and as long as they did they had little difficulty in handling important issues of life. But soon

---

[6]    *Culture*, 291.
[7]    "Arnold Dolmetsch", *Pavannes and Divisions*, 143-144.

the belief in objectivity and the confidence in mass knowledge grew stronger and upset the traditional mode of perception. A small number of people who still kept the old way had now to turn into myth-makers – poets and artists. They composed "an impersonal or objective story woven out of his own emotion, as the nearest equation that he was capable of putting into words", since this was the only way in which they could communicate their perception to others.

It is worth noting that Pound, like Yeats, accuses objective-minded men of losing the right approach to truth, but that he, unlike Yeats, does not reject natural science itself as valueless or misleading. On the contrary Pound thinks highly of science because of its impersonal, precise method. In fact he goes even so far as to define art in terms of science:

The arts, literature, poesy, are a science, just as chemistry is a science. Their subject is man, mankind and the individual. The subject of chemistry is matter considered as to its composition.
The arts give us a great percentage of the lasting and unassailable data regarding the nature of man, of immaterial man, of man considered as a thinking and sentient creature. They begin where the science of medicine leaves off or rather they overlap that science. The borders of the two arts overcross.
From medicine we learn that man thrives best when duly washed, aired and sunned. From the arts we learn that man is whimsical, that one man differs from another. That men differ among themselves as leaves upon trees differ. That they do not resemble each other as do buttons cut by machine.[8]

Art and science differ only in the areas which their subject-matters cover; while the subject of the latter is natural objects (man included) and phenomena, that of the former is man, or human mind. Science gives us exact data for determining what sort of world man lives in; art provides us with best data for deciding what sort of creature man is. This is the only difference between the two – and even this difference is very vague along the borderline. In all the other aspects an artist and a scientist work in the same way, and their highest aim is to be faithful to actual experience, to collect and give precise

"The Serious Artist", *Pavannes and Divisions*, 220.

data in their respective fields. "The serious artist", Pound says, "is scientific in that he presents the image of his desire, of his hate, of his indifference as precisely that, as precisely the image of his own desire, hate or indifference. The more precise his record the more lasting and unassailable his work of art."[9] What an artist and a scientist must avoid is to turn into a theoretician. A theorist's judgement, whether scientific or artistic, is usually unsound because it is "empiric in the medieval fasion", because it is far removed from immediate experience.

A good artist, then, is a person who makes an accurate report on man. But what sort of things about man should the artist report? Pound give a rather loose itemization of the artist's subject-matter in a passage where he criticizes the inaccurate artist:

If an artist falsifies his report as to the nature of man, as to his own desire, as to the nature of his ideal of the perfect, as to the nature of his ideal of this, that or the other, of god, if god exists, of the life force, of the nature of good and evil, if good and evil exist, of the force with which he believes or disbelieves this, that or the other, of the degree in which he suffers or is made glad; if the artist falsifies his reports on these matters or on any other matter in order that he may conform to the taste of his time, to the properties of a sovereign, to the conveniences of a preconceived code of ethics, then that artist lies.[10]

It is characteristic of Pound that he does not say in a Yeatsian manner that the dominant themes of art are Man, God, Immortality, or something of this sort. For Pound the subject of art is all-inclusive: man as he is, man as he should be, nature, god, life-force, good and evil, etc., etc. The important thing is that the artist's report must be accurate: bad art is inaccurate art, a bad artist is a false reporter, and whether he falsifies his report out of deliberate will, out of carelessness, out of cowardice, or out of laziness, he is dishonest and should be punished. The issue is not what he believes in but how he

---

[9]    *Ibid.*, 226.
[10]    *Ibid.*, 222-223.

reports his belief. Here the accuracy of the artist's report becomes a matter of ethics, since art, providing data for our
conception of what man is, constitutes the core of ethics.

However, to attain the maximum accuracy in artistic creation is no easy task. Any of the themes of art enumerated in
the last quotation is large and complex. If one wants to express
simple desires, one has only to say "food", "water" or "fire".
When one wants to convey an idea, one must have recourse
to speech; the more complex the idea, the more complex the
speech. But one may go a step further: one may wish to communicate an idea and its modifications, an idea and a crowd
of its effects. One may wish to question whether a certain
formula works in every case, or in what percentage of cases,
and so forth. Then one gets the Henry James novel.[11] Or, in
the case of poetry:

You wish to communicate an idea and its concomitant emotions, or
an emotion and its concomitant ideas, or a sensation and its deriva-
tive emotions, or an impression that is emotive, etc. etc. etc. You
begin with the yeowl and the bark, and you develop into the dance
and into music, and into music with words, and finally into words
with music, and finally into words with a vague adumbration of
music, words suggestive of music, words measured, or words in a
rhythm that preserves some accurate trait of the emotive impression, or of the sheer character of the fostering or parental emotion.[12]

Pound makes a distinction between the emotion felt by the
poet and the emotion embodied in the poem; the one belongs
to life, and the other to art. A person tries to reproduce his
emotion so that it will be shared with his fellow men, but it
usually is so complex that mere speech is not enough; he needs
technique – art. Artistic technique is the very thing that gives
accuracy to a most advanced kind of communication.

This distinction between life-feeling and aesthetic emotion
is one of Pound's keen insights which gives depth and scope
to his notion of communication. Art imitates life, but in the
process of imitation life goes through a metamorphosis; life is

[11]   *Ibid.*, 233.
[12]   *Ibid.*, 233-234.

given form and order. "Any work of art is a compound of freedom and order", says Pound. "It is perfectly obvious that art hangs between chaos on one side and mechanics on the other."[13] In other words, a work of art consists of subject-matter and form, the former provided by life and the latter given by the artist. One should never mistake the one for the other; if one does, one will fall into a delusion in which one thinks all works of art dealing with a beautiful object are beautiful. Popular artists are fond of treating beautiful objects for their subject-matter; as a result, their works are sentimental or "caressable", and not beautiful. "Our respect is not for the subject-matter, but for the creative power of the artist", Pound warns, "for that which he is capable of adding to his subject from himself; or, in fact, his capacity to dispense with external subjects altogether, to create from himself or from elements".[14] The satisfactions of art are different from satisfactions of life; the former is more lofty than the latter, or beyond the latter. In Rodin's "La Vieille Heaulmière", for example, the subject is "hideous"; it is grief for the loss of youth, intensified by a title reminiscent of Villon; and, so far as the emotional effect is concerned, scarcely anyone will deny that Villon's poem is more efficient than the statue. The fact is that the beauty of the statue depends in no appreciable degree on the subject. The beauty is from Rodin. It is in the composition, particularly in the silhouettes.

If the artist's task lies in an accurate communication of his feeling, the most important thing for him is to discover a fresh and individual form which will perfectly fit his emotion. No two individuals feel in the same way, and each individual feeling requires a different mode of expression. Every act of poetic creation is to find an equation to human emotions; poetry, in this sense, is inspired mathematics. In fact, the nature of poetry will become clearer by analogy with the four different intensities of mathematical expression: the arithmetical, the algebraic, the geometrical, and analytical

[13]  "Arnold Dolmetsch", *Pavannes and Divisions*, 258.
[14]  *Gaudier Brzeska*, 114-115.

geometry. On the simplest level there is an arithmetical equation:

$$3 \times 3 + 4 \times 4 = 5 \times 5$$

or $$3^2 + 4^2 = 5^2$$

Any ordinary man knows this; it is common sense. We collect a few more examples:

$$3^2 + 4^2 = 5^2; 6^2 + 8^2 = 10^2; 9^2 + 12^2 = 15^2; \ldots$$

and arrive at:

$$a^2 + b^2 = c^2$$

This is an equation which stands for all individual cases. It is the method of philosophy; indeed, philosophy consists of such equations. But then we can think of $a$, $b$ and $c$ as three sides of a right-angled triangle, and of $a^2$, $b^2$ and $c^2$ as three squares which stand on them. Here we have come to the question of form; it is like art criticism. Then finally we get to analytical geometry. We set up two axes, horizontal (x) and vertical (y), and draw a circle governed by:

$$(x - a)^2 + (y - b)^2 = r^2$$

It is not a particular circle; it is any circle and all circles. It is nothing that is not a circle. It is the circle free of space and time elements; it is the universal, existing in perfection. "It is in this way", Pound says, "that art handles life. The difference between art and analytical geometry is the difference of subject-matter only. Art is more interesting in proportion as life and the human consciousness are more complex and more interesting than forms and numbers."[15] The concept, expounded in an essay written in 1914, clearly anticipates Eliot's idea of "objective correlative".

A work of art, then, is an equation which presents a truth, or a part of truth, as conceived through intellect and emotion. If there is such a thing as the supreme intelligence of the uni-

[15]  *Ibid.*, 106.

verse, art is "an emphasis, a segregation of some component of that intelligence for the sake of making it more perceptible".[16] The artist's task is twofold: first, a firm grasp of what he is to communicate, and second, an accurate expression of what he has grasped. Art is interpretative and communicative. And interpretation and communication are dependent on each other: one cannot make any accurate report of a fact without having interpreted it with precision, nor can one mould chaos into order without some system of expression. Good art is accurate communication, and accurate communication consists of exact interpretation and precise expression.

It is for this reason that Pound, who seems so much concerned with literary form, never neglects to emphasize the importance of content. "The best poetry", he declares, "has always a content."[17] He makes a distinction between pre- and post-Renaissance literature in favor of the former, and says that while the writers before Arthur Golding were all intent on what they were saying, the authors after him became more concerned with the way they were saying it.[18] Pope is dull, because a good deal of him is not informative.[19] The aesthetes since 1880 are not "a very sturdy lot" for the same reason. In contrast, such writers as Homer, Dante, Villon and Omar are great because they are saying something, because they are "didactic"; a revelation is always "didactic".[20] Pound warns against confusing "profounder didacticism" with literary propaganda. Propagandist literature always starts with a ready-made solution; it belongs to the era of theology and dogma.[21] Literature with "profounder didacticism" is based on a free examination of the data, with no reference to a particular creed or theory; if it comes to assume a great propagandist value, this is purely accidental on the writer's part. "The artist is free", Pound repeatedly emphasizes. "The true artist

[16]  *Culture*, 189-190.
[17]  "A Study in French Poets", *Instigations*, 72.
[18]  *The ABC of Reading*, 117-118.
[19]  *Ibid.*, 157-158.
[20]  Letter to Felix E. Schelling, 1922. *Letters*, 180.

is the champion of free speech from the beginning."[22] "He must be as free as the mathematician."[23] "The serious artist must be as open as nature."[24] Anyone can be a good artist only if he faces with an open mind an object which sufficiently interests him. "If", Pound says, "another man has ideas of *any* kind (not borrowed cliches) that irritate you enough to make you think or take out your own ideas and look at 'em, that is all one can expect".[25] The making of a poem is as simple as all that. One does not have to have an elaborate system of philosophy or metaphysics; one has only to interpret a slice of human reality in one's own way; one has only to "discover the truth, or a part of the truth, even before one has learned that it may not be the whole truth."[26] The artist may have any and every thought and opinion as long as he perceives truth in it. "The force of a work of art is this", Pound writes, "namely, that the artist presents his case, as fully or as minutely as he may choose".[27] Even the artist's motive does not matter, whether it be his desire for the good of the race or his personal vanity. The most important is that his work has a vital force coming from its truth, from its interpretative power. "An art is vital", Pound sums up, "only so far as it is interpretative, so long, that is, as it manifests something which the artist perceives at greater intensity, and more intimately, than his public. If he be the seeing man among the sightless, they will attend him so long as his statements seem, or are proven, true."[28] One of the basic points of difference between the artist and the average man lies in the power of interpretation.

Art, as an interpretation of life, is a mode of perception. It is most urgently needed when life is inarticulate and apparently without design, that is, "when the conclusion or results of

[21] "Open Letter to Tretyakow", *Impact*, 227.
[22] *Patria Mia*, 78.
[23] *Ibid.*, 39.
[24] *Ibid.*, 40.
[25] Letter to James Vogel, 1929. *Letters*, 222.
[26] "A Visiting Card", *Impact*, 59.
[27] *Patria Mia*, 77.
[28] "Psychology and Troubadours", *The Spirit of Romance*, 87.

given causes are so far removed or so hidden, that art alone can show their relation".[29] "Cranks and doctrinaires" try to do the same thing, but what they actually do is to propagate some specific details of a fixed system, often without understanding the system itself. Artists are not confined within a system; their mind is free and attempts to broaden others' mind through their work. "A work of art", Pound says: "Any serious work vivifies a man's total perception of relations."[30] An artist is a medium in the sense that he perceives what an average man does not; a work of art is also a medium since it is through the work that the artist or the reader perceives the imperceptible. There are two kinds of artists, depending upon whether the stress falls on the former case or the latter. The one is the philosophical artist to whom art is a medium, a means of self-expression; the other is the mediumistic artist who can only exist in his art, who is passive to impulse. The faculty of this second type, as Pound thinks, is most useful as a part of the complete artist's equipment.[31] When the latter kind of artist is in his mediumistic function, people say he is in a trance or in madness; but in reality he is in a state of "ecstasy", "a glow arising from the exact nature of the perception".[32] In the former kind of artist one may say that art is subject to the will of the artist; in the latter art gets beyond it. Here we feel tempted to associate the former with the classicists' insistence on self-restraint and style, and to connect the latter to the romantics' mystic way of perception. Pound, however, prefers to define classicism and romanticism in terms of artistic effects. "Speaking generally", he says, "the spells or equations of 'classic' art invoke the beauty of the normal, and spells of 'romantic' art are said to invoke the beauty of the unusual."[33]

The most basic function of the artist is interpretation, but there is another function just as important and essential –

[29] "Camoens", *The Spirit of Romance*, 218.
[30] "History and Ignorance", *Impact*, 237.
[31] *Gaudier Brzeska*, 125.
[32] "Psychology and Troubadours", *The Spirit of Romance*, 91.
[33] "The Phantom Dawn", *The Spirit of Romance*, 14.

communication. The artist must know how to make the most precise report on what he has interpreted. This is the question of technique, of precision in technique. As we have already pointed out, Pound is most concerned with "precision" wherever he talks about the technique of poetry. By "precision" he means "maximum efficiency of expression". "I mean", says he, "that the writer has expressed something interesting in such a way that one cannot resay it more effectively."[34] Interpretation is primarily subjective, and a conviction implied in it cannot be refuted. But technique is objective; one who makes imprecise presentation of his observation is either a poor technician or an insincere artist. In fact, if the artist is not a precise technician, how can one distinguish his statements from those of a lunatic? Because his utterance is accurate, the interested reader can "interpret, more or less, the artists' ambiguous, or more than ambiguous, verbal statements about life, cosmos, being, non-being, time, eternity, etc.".[35] When one says: "Send me four pounds of ten-penny nails", the meaning is quite clear to any listener. But when one says: "Send me the kind of Rembrandt I like", the meaning is ambiguous. It is ambiguous not because the language is ambiguous but because the idea implied in the statement is ambiguous. A poet's task is to say "Send me the kind of Rembrandt I like" in language which will render the meaning as clear as "Send me four pounds of ten-penny nails".[36]

One way to create precise language is to avoid the use of abstract words. The artist is all right so long as he sticks to words as simple as dog, horse and sunset, but his communication ceases almost entirely when he writes down "good", "evil", or "proper".[37] Importance of simple diction cannot be over-emphasized. "The true poet", Pound says, "is most easily distinguished from the false, when he trusts himself to the simplest expression, and when he writes without adjectives."[38]

[34]   "The Serious Artist", *Pavannes and Divisions*, 240-241.
[35]   "George Antheil", *Antheil and the Treatise on Harmony*, 40-41.
[36]   "The Serious Artist", *Pavannes and Divisions*, 233.
[37]   *Culture*, 48-49.
[38]   "The Quality of Lope de Vega", *The Spirit of Romance*, 208.

Victorian poetry had been filled with abstract and superfluous words like "dim land of peace", until Yeats came out and "boiled away all that is not poetic – and a good deal that is".[39] Use either no ornament or good ornament.[40] The poetry of the future will move against "poppycock", it will be harder and saner, it will be "nearer the bone".[41] Avoid rhetoric on one hand, and shun the levelling of style on the other. *Of* and *-ing* are useless syllables; every syllable should have a reason for being there.[42] Even in translating a literary work, the translator should leave out all unnecessary words even though they appear in the original – that is, the words "not necessary to the meaning of the *whole* passage, any whole passage".[43] Pound concludes:

Roughly then, good writing is writing that is perfectly controlled, the writer says just what he means. He says it with complete clarity and simplicity. He uses the smallest possible number of words. I do not mean that he skimps paper, or that he screws about like Tacitus to get his thought crowded into the least possible space. But, granting that two sentences are at times easier to understand than one sentence containing the double meaning, the author tries to communicate with the reader with the greatest possible despatch, save where for any one of forty reasons he does not wish to do so.[44]

This is as simple as the sculptor's direction: "Take a chisel and cut away all the stone you don't want."[45]

This concept of precision and economy in the use of language becomes a definition of literature itself. "Literature is language charged with meaning", writes Pound. "Great literature is simply language charged with meaning to the utmost possible degree."[46] Every poetic technique, in its final analysis, is an attempt to charge language with meaning to the

---

[39] "A Retrospect", *Pavannes and Divisions*, 107.
[40] "A Stray Document", *Make It New*, 338.
[41] "A Retrospect", *Pavannes and Divisions*, 107-108.
[42] Letter to Mary Barnard, 1934. *Letters*, 261.
[43] Letter to W. H. D. Rouse, 1935. *Letters*, 269.
[44] "The Serious Artist", *Pavannes and Divisions*, 232.
[45] Letter to Iris Barry, 1916. *Letters*, 91.
[46] *The ABC of Reading*, 12.

greatest possible degree. Roughly speaking, there are three ways to charge language with meaning:

MELOPOEIA, wherein the words are charged, over and above their plain meaning, with some musical property, which directs the bearing or trend of that meaning.

PHANOPOEIA, which is a casting of images upon the visual imagination.

LOGOPOEIA, "the dance of the intellect among words", that is to say, it employs words not only for their direct meaning, but it takes count in a special way of habits of usage, of the context we *expect* to find with the word, its usual concomitants, of its known accept-ances, and of ironical play. It holds the aesthetic content which is peculiarly the domain of verbal manifestation, and cannot possibly be contained in plastic or in music. It is the latest come, and perhaps most tricky and undependable mode.[47]

Almost all of Pound's comments on the techniques of poetry are related to one or another of these three methods of literary composition. We shall examine them in some detail, but before doing so we need to clarify the basis on which these distinctions are made.

In brief, what provides the basis is "the primary form" as Pound calls it. In his opinion, every creative thought is con-crete; it is "a sudden outspurt of mind which takes the form demanded by the problem".[48] It is not that the poet thinks first in abstraction and then moulds his thought into concrete things. He thinks and feels among concrete things from the first. His writing is conterminous with his thought; it has the form of the thought, "the form of the way the man feels his thought".[49] This is true of every art: "Every concept, every emotion presents itself to the vivid consciousness in some pri-mary form. It belongs to the art of this form. If sound, to music; if formed words, to literature; the image, to poetry; form, to design; colour in position, to painting; form or design in three planes, to sculpture; movement, to the dance or to the

[47]   "How to Read", *Polite Essays*, 170.
[48]   "Postscript to *The Natural Philosophy of Love* by Remy de Gourmont", *Pavannes and Divigations*, 208.
[49]   *The ABC of Reading*, 99.

rhythm of music or verses."[50] The passage was written in 1916, when Pound was an enthusiastic member of the vorticist group. Consequently he uses "poetry" in a narrow sense of his own: it is vorticist poetry, as against "literature and verse". In this narrow sense, then, the primary form of "poetry" is image (phanopoeia), that of "verse" is movement (melopoeia), and that of "literature" is formed words (logopoeia). But literature, in its broader and normal sense (which includes Pound's "poetry", "verse" and "literature"), would have all the three primary forms. If the emotion which comes up to the poet's consciousness is of visual kind, he will compose an imagistic poem. If the emotion appeals to his auditory imagination with its rhythm and melody, he will create a lyric poem. If the emotion is more complex and intellectual, the poet will write a poem of irony. All depends upon the way in which thought or emotion first presents itself to the conscious mind of the artist.

In melopoeia, therefore, the primary emotion is musical; every emotion or every phase of emotion has some sort of "rhythm-phrase" to express it. This may be called "absolute rhythm", since it belongs to that particular emotion alone. "I believe", says Pound, "in an 'absolute rhythm', a rhythm, that is, in poetry which corresponds exactly to the emotion or shade of emotion to be expressed."[51] If the poet is to express the emotion most precisely, he has no way but to render this rhythm into his verse. Naturally the rhythm will not conform to any of the ready-made meters, because it is internal, because it is inherent in the particular emotion of a particular poet. This necessitated *vers libre*. The rhythm of a *vers libre* poem is the rhythm of the primary emotion which the poem contains. The poet, therefore, must be extremely cautious in using the *vers libre* form; he should not use it unless he is forced to. Pound repeatedly warns against a misapplied or excessive use of *vers libre*: "I think one should write vers libre only when one 'must', that is to say, only when the 'thing'

---

[50]  *Gaudier Brzeska*, 93.
[51]  "A Retrospect", *Pavannes and Divisions*, 103.

builds up a rhythm more beautiful than that of set metres, or more real, more a part of the emotion of the 'thing', more germane, intimate, interpretative than the measure of regular accentual verse."[52] No beginner in verse-writing should try a hand in *vers libre*; only those who have good mastery in regular verse-forms can do competent work in *vers libre*.

All this is merely to say that there is practically no difference between *vers libre* and conventional verse in principle; both try to register or suggest an emotional phenomenon which cannot otherwise be expressed. This is also the aim of music; here poetry comes very close to music. Music can do what ordinary words cannot do: it is "the bridge between consciousness and the unthinking sentient or even insentient universe".[53] Melopoeia may be understood as poetry on the border of music, or "music just forcing itself into articulate speech".[54] A good poet, therefore, is always a good musician too. "In short", Pound advises, "behave as a musician, a good musician, when dealing with that phase of your art which has exact parallels in music. The same laws govern, and you are bound by no others."[55] A poet, like a musician, is an expert in handling time and time relations; he delimits them in an interesting manner, by means of longer and shorter, heavier and lighter syllables, and the varying qualities of sound inseparable from the words of his speech.[56] Just as a musician knows harmony and counterpoint and all the minutiae of his craft, a poet should know assonance and alliteration, various kinds of rhymes, and all other details of metrics, even though he may seldom have need of them.[57] It is not necessary for a poem to rely on its music; but, if it is melopoeia and does rely on music, that music must be such as will delight the expert.

In contrast with melopoeia, phanopoeia presupposes imagery for its primary emotion. As Pound maintains, certain

[52]   *Ibid.*, 108.
[53]   "How to Read", *Polite Essays*, 172.
[54]   "The Later Yeats", *Literary Essays*, 380.
[55]   "A Stray Document", *Make It New*, 339.
[56]   *The ABC of Reading*, 189.
[57]   "A Stray Document", *Make It New*, 338.

emotions or ideas, when they come up to a person's consciousness and before he can formulate them in words, appeal to his
inner vision. These visual "pre-thoughts" often lie beyond
the existing categories of language, just as certain colors or
shades of colors in nature cannot be designated by the existing
names of colors. When a person has one of these emotions or
ideas, he is capable of expressing it only through visual imagery; the image is his "primary pigment", the first adequate
equation that has come into his consciousness.[58] If such an
experience is made into a poem, it will become an imagist
poem.

Pound's idea of the image, seemingly unique and modern,
may be traced back to the Romantic tradition of Western
poetry. He analyzes the poet's image-forming process in the
objective manner of modern psychology, but on the top of
it he imposes his own evaluative judgement of intellect and
emotion, the conscious and the subconscious. Just as Blake
and Coleridge emphasize the function of the Imagination in
the process of perceiving truth, Pound cherishes "pre-thought"
rather than thought, the "primary pigment" rather than the
finished picture. An emotion or idea, when it is still in the
subconscious, is completely unique and free since the gene-
ralizing power of intellect does not reach it; but, as soon as it
crosses the border into the conscious, it begins to harden.
Words and phrases, in their effort to define it, tend to kill its
freshness and vitality since they are conventional and inevitably have dead parts. In phanopoeia the poet tries to retain
maximum vitality of his perception by minimizing the discursive function of language – that is, by the use of the image.
As Frank Kermode observes, one may say Pound and the
imagists wished that poetry could be written with something
other than words, but since this was impossible they attempted
to make words having the same sort of physical presence "as a
piece of string".[59] This "thingness" of the image is mainly
what distinguishes Pound from the traditional Englsih roman-

---

[58] Cf. Frank Kermode, *The Romantic Image*, 119-137.
[59] *Gaudier Brzeska*, 97.

tics. In Burns and Shelley, for example, the poetic image is a medium which introduces the reader into a dim realm of infinity; Pound, on the other hand, emphasizes the finiteness of the image, the precision and clarity of the vision. In traditional romanticism the individual unconscious is tied with the collective memory of the race; in Pound it is not so.

In its anti-intellectual nature Pound's concept of the image has naturally much in common with the symbolists', who, after all, are the followers of Romanticism, too. But Pound's insistence on the individuality of the image breaks him away from the symbolists. As Pound feels, a symbolist poet uses an image to present a perception which, though it may not be intellectual or discursive, is historical, mythical, or at any rate pre-determined. Pound calls this sort of image a "symbol". The function of the "symbol", therefore, depends on conventional association, allusion or allegory; the symbolist would use, for instance, the term "cross" to mean "trial". The symbolist's "symbols" have a fixed value, like numbers in arithmetic, like 1, 2, and 7. The imagist's images have a variable significance, like the signs $a$, $b$ and $x$ in algebra. [60] The "symbol" evokes merely a set of conventional ideas in the reader's mind. The image, on the other hand, liberates the reader from them:

An "Image" is that which presents an intellectual and emotional complex in an instant of time. ... It is the presentation of such a "complex" instantaneously which gives that sense of sudden liberation; that sense of freedom from time limits and space limits; that sense of sudden growth, which we experience in the presence of the greatest works of art. [61]

The image is a catalyzer, something that promotes and accelerates a chemical combination, itself not participating in the process directly. The poet's task is to discover such a catalyzer, rather than to attempt to state his case by rhetorical means. Dante is great because he has created the most wonderful image, "Paradiso", whereas Milton is a "windbag"

[60]    *Gaudier Brzeska*, 97.
[61]    "A Stray Document", *Make It New*, 336.

because he depends on rhetoric. The image is the farthest possible remove from rhetoric.[62] One says "I am" this, that, or the other, and with the words scarcely uttered one ceases to be that thing. The poet should, as a Russian correspondent once remarked, try to "give people new eyes, not to make them see some new particular thing".[63] The image, or the imagist poem, provides new eyes.

How to compose an imagist poem is set forth in the well-known imagist manifestoes of 1912 and 1915. Pound's example, a "hokku-like sentence":

> The apparition of these faces in the crowd:
> Petals, on a wet, black bough.

has become famous, too. One thing worth mentioning here, however, is the fact that the image as conceived by Pound, is not static but moving. In the poem cited above, for instance, the relation between the two images is not a mere parallel or juxtaposition. The image of the faces at the subway station and that of petals on a bough have no logical or associational connection with each other; they are not "symbols" which stand for some abstract value or which evoke some historical or mythical associations. They are purely sensory images, and the poem, in this sense, is objective. But when we read the poem we find that the latter image, that of petals on a bough, acts upon the former and creates a certain sensory impression in our mind. People's white faces are moving in a confused stream on the dirty, dimly lighted platform of a subway station. They are beautiful in a strange way. The unique quality of this beauty cannot be defined or described in ordinary explanatory words. So Pound brings in the image of petals on a wet, black bough and super-imposes it over the image of faces in the crowd. The latter image, with its feeling of pale and delicate yet animated loveliness, covers the former image and gives it a clear delineation. The face image actively responds to the flower image which falls upon it with full

[62]  *Gaudier Brzeska*, 95.
[63]  *Ibid.*, 98.

force. This kind of vital interaction between images is essential to an imagist poem. And the whole poem must have a unity which is provided by the central image. It is like a whirlpool, various kinds of images, emotions and ideas going round and round pointing toward a center. The image, as Pound says, is a radiant node or cluster. "It is", he goes on, "what I can, and must perforce, call a VORTEX, from which, and through which, and into which, ideas are constantly rushing." Imagism now becomes vorticism.[64] This technique is adopted, Pound observes, in some of the best *nō* plays, in which the unity of the drama consists in one image. Pound himself employs the technique in many parts of his *Cantos*.[65]

Pound's insistence on the image or vortex as a method of poetry leads to his enthusiasm for Chinese ideograph. He first became interested in Chinese ideograph when he came across a manuscript by Ernest Fenollosa, which he later edited and published under the title "The Chinese Written Character as a Medium for Poetry". He thought highly of the essay; he even called it "a study of the fundamentals of all aesthetics", and made it the guiding principle of his *ABC of Reading*. The central thesis of the essay is rather simple: as against Western languages which describe an object or action in abstract terms, Chinese ideograph presents the thing in visual imagery. In the West a person who wants to define a thing always describes it in more and more general terms, receding from definite, concrete things into more and more imprecise, unknown areas; he would, for example, define "red" as "color", as "a vibration or a refraction of light", then as "a division of the spectrum", and so forth. Yet, as Fenollosa and Pound think, a true noun does not exist in nature; things are only "the terminal points, or rather the meeting points of actions, cross-sections cut through actions, snap-shots". Neither can a pure verb, an abstract motion, be possible in nature; for we always see noun and verb as one: things in motion, motion in things.

[64]   *Ibid.*, 106.
[65]   Cf. Earl Miner, *The Japanese Tradition in British and American Literature*, 108-155.

Chinese characters represent things in motion, and motion in things. They can do this because they are constructed out of small abbreviated picture-units which spontaneously appeal to our eyes, and which act upon one another to create one concrete concept as a whole. Thus the sun underlying the bursting forth of plants signifies spring; the sun sign tangled in the branches of the tree sign is east.

The method of ideograph is the basic principle of the technique of phanopoeia. Art and poetry, attempting to present a concrete truth as man sees it, deal with concrete nature; they shy away from the abstract and the general which do not exist in nature. Therefore, the more concretely and vividly we express the interactions of things, the better poetry we shall have. "We need in poetry thousands of active words, each doing its utmost to show forth the motive and vital forces", says Pound (for this is Pound's, and not Fenollosa's, characteristic style). "We cannot exhibit the wealth of nature by mere summation, by the piling of sentences. Poetic thought works by suggestion, crowding maximum meaning into the single phrase pregnant, charged, and luminous from within."[66] Chinese language, which makes this its function, is most poetic; we should try to imitate it in our verse-writing too. The present decay of Western poetry has its roots back in Greek philosophy which was mostly "a mere splitting, an impoverishment of understanding". Socrates was "a distinguished gas-bag" in comparison with Confucius and Mencius.[67]

Pound's understanding of Chinese ideograph contains many irrelevant facts and misconceived ideas, whether they originally come from Fenollosa or from himself.[68] Nevertheless, his concept of ideographic method in verse-writing is no doubt valid. In a sense it is nothing new or original, since his ideographic method is basically no different from the idea of

[66]  "Chinese Written Character", *Instigations*, 382-383.
[67]  Letter to Katsue Kitasono, 1940. *Letters*, 347.
[68]  Cf. Hugh Gordon Porteus, "Ezra Pound and His Chinese Character a Radical Examination", *An Examination of Ezra Pound*, 203-217.

the complex image, metaphor and symbol in the Romantic tradition of the West. A complex metaphor (Pound's "image" and Yeats's "symbol") presents multiple levels of meaning, imaginatively related to each other and harmoniously united in a concrete image, or in a series of concrete images. This is precisely what Pound's ideographic method does (provided, of course, that the method is successfully applied). The poet will toss out lines with a number of heterogeneous images corresponding to different parts of an ideograph, yet he will see to it that these images form a unity of meaning as a whole just as an ideograph has a definite meaning in itself. In the first book of *Paradise Lost*, for example, the poet sets forth a cluster of different images around Satan – a Titan, Typhon, Leviathan, an island on the ocean. In *Canto* LXXX Pound presents a series of images – the "moon nymph" of a *nō* play *Hagoromo*, Diana, the Holy Spirit, Venus – seemingly unrelated yet really pointing toward the unifying image of a heavenly visitor to the earth. Although Pound would loathe to have his method compared with Milton's, the two methods seem to be fundamentally the same, the difference being only in the degree of logical relationship between the images.

But, from another point of view, this difference in degree is important. In Milton (and in the poets and playwrights before him) the poetic image always had a logical structure at its bottom, in addition to its associational make-up. Anyone can readily recognize a logical connection among a Titan, Typhon, Leviathan and a large island; they are all huge in bulk and can be formidable to those who carelessly approach them. But how many of us can off-hand identify the heroine of *Hagoromo* in reading Pound's lines and associate her with Diana, the Holy Spirit and Venus? Here the poet is depending solely upon the associational faculty of the reader, with no sure guarantee that the average reader will not fail to grasp the associational connection. Pound, in this respect, is the latest development of the Western Romantic tradition which came to occupy the central position in English poetry after Milton's time. The romantics, as we have observed, sought a truth unreachable through discursive reason, a truth which the poet's imagination alone can get hold of. The image thus became more and more private and personal; it depended more and more on association rather than on logic. This trend resulted in the isolation of the artist from common humanity on the one hand, and in the increasing obscurity of poetic meaning on the other. It was enhanced by the Symbolist movement and came to flourish in contemporary poetry. The image has now become "pseudo-reference", as Yvor Winters terms it: having no or little denotative meaning, it refers to either non-existent or extremely obscure motivation or symbolic value.[69] In the same way Pound's image minimizes or cripples its discursive function; his ideographic method makes little attempt at a rational progression. His image, in this respect, does differ from the pre-romantic and anti-romantic metaphor or symbol.

Pound has far less to say about logopoeia than about melopoeia or phanopoeia. The reason perhaps is that Pound thinks it the "most tricky and undependable mode" among the three. He himself confesses that he, as a poet, is surpassed by T. S. Eliot in this category, although he is better than Eliot in melopoeia.[70] Whereas the primary emotions of melopoeia and phanopoeia manifest themselves through sound and imagery respectively, logopoeia presupposes certain kinds of emotions which can be expressed only by verbal means. In this case, the poet will arrange his words in such a way that they act on each other's meaning and themselves assume some special meaning and tone in that particular context; this stands on the same principle with which the musical composer or the painter cuts time or space into some peculiar pattern of his own. In other words, the basic principle of logopoeia is irony – irony in its broadest sense.

The essential quality of irony is oppositeness. Ironic utterance states, not the expected, but the unexpected, and even the contrary of what is expected. When used by the poet, irony

[69]  Cf. Yvor Winters, *In Defense of Reason*, 40-64.
[70]  "A Visiting Card", *Impact*, 59.

serves to make a complex statement with precision, for it
provides multiplicity of meaning on the one hand and individuality of statement on the other. Each word has its universal
or denotative meaning; but the poet, by using it in some
special (and often contrary) relation to the ordinary usage,
gives it his particular or connotative signification. The reader,
while having in mind the universal meaning of the word, is
suddenly confronted with the special connotation of the word
particularized by the context of the poem. In other words,
the reader is instantly made aware that what is opposite on one
level is apposite on another. Thus there occurs in his mind a
complex intellectual interaction between the thing said and the
thing anticipated, which immediately stimulates his associational faculty and makes his mind active. Pound's way of
saying this is that the words start "a play or 'dance' among the
concomitant meanings, customs, usages, and implied contexts
of the words themselves".[71] The idea is essentially the same as
that of melopoeia and phanopoeia: the difference is only in the
kind of stimulus which starts the "dance". The stimulus is
rhythm in melopoeia and imagery in phanopoeia: in logopoeia it is intellect, which is far more efficiently presented
through words than through music or painting. So Pound's
another name for logopoeia is "verbalism", in contrast with
lyricism and imagism. Since language is most intrinsically
involved in logopoeia, the method is most complex and risky;
it can only be used by the sophisticated.[72] For the same reason
logopoeia cannot be translated into a foreign tongue.

It is very likely that Pound learned the idea of logopoeia
through Jules Laforgue. "Unless I am right in discovering
*logopoeia* in Propertius ...", writes Pound, "we must almost
say that Laforgue invented *logopoeia* – observing that there had
been a very limited range of *logopoeia* in all satire, and that
Heine occasionally employs something like it ... At any rate
Laforgue found or refound *logopoeia*."[73] The instances of

[71]   *Ibid.*, 59.
[72]   *The ABC of Reading*, 22.
[73]   *How to Read*, 33.

Pound's irony in the vein of Laforgue which appear in his poetry, particularly in *Hugh Selwyn Mauberley*, have been pointed out by Warren Ramsey and John J. Espey.[74] But it seems that Pound thought of irony as a principle not only of one particular type of poetry but of poetry in general. It might even be suggested that he anticipates I. A. Richards who interprets poetic experience as the equilibrium of opposed impulses, or Cleanth Brooks who holds that irony brings forth "the stability of a context in which the internal pressures balance and mutually support each other".[75] Although they put it in different idioms, they all seem to share the opinion that words in a poem must be related in such a way that each accurately defines others. Irony, which each word comes to assume under the pressure of the context, provides objectivity and precision for a poetic statement.

Examining Pound's three ways of charging language with meaning, one may wonder whether he is talking of poetry alone, poetry exclusive of prose fiction or drama. His own attitude toward the issue is rather ambivalent. One thing, however, is clear: the language of prose is much less highly charged with meaning than that of poetry.[76] Sometimes Pound seems to think quite lightly of the difference. "But these things are relative", he writes. "Just as we say that a certain temperature is hot and another cold. ... The thing that counts is 'Good Writing'".[77] Particularly during the last century or century and a half prose has arisen to challenge the poetic pre-eminence.[78] But at other times Pound seems to believe that the difference between poetry and prose is in kind rather than in degree. For example, he says: "In the verse something has come upon the intelligence. In the prose the intelligence has found a subject for its observations. The poetic

---

[74] Cf. Warren Ramsey, *Jules Laforgue and the Ironic Inheritance*, 204-212; John J. Espey, *Ezra Pound's Mauberley*, 63-66.
[75] Cf. Cleanth Brooks, "Irony as a Principle of Structure", *Literary Opinion in America*, 732-733.
[76] "How to Read", *Polite Essays*, 171.
[77] "The Serious Artist", *Pavannes and Divisions*, 231.
[78] "How to Read", *Polite Essays*, 171.

fact pre-exists."[79] The prose-writer observes things and describes them in logical terms, but the poet presents his intellectual or emotional perception in logical and illogical terms. The
difference is essential, and one is justified in raising a doubt
whether poetry is part of literature. True poetry is in much
closer relation to the best of music, of painting and of sculpture,
than to any part of literature which is not true poetry. For:

The spirit of the arts is dynamic. The arts are not passive, nor
static, nor, in s sense, are they reflective, though reflection may
assist at their birth.
    Poetry is about as much a "criticism of life" as red-hot iron is a
criticism of fire.[80]

If Matthew Arnold considered poetry as part of literature, his
definition of literature as criticism of life is "the one notable
blasphemy that was born of his mind's frigidity".

    In Pound's opinion, therefore, the relation of poetry (as
distinct from "literature") to other arts is a very close one. All
arts have emotional intensity, vital energy, the quality of red-
hot iron – in Pound's metaphor "a force transfusing, welding,
and unifying" or "a force rather like water when it spurts up
through very bright sand and sets it in swift motion".[81] What
differentiates one art from another is, as we have already
observed, the "primary emotion". A good work of art will
embody an emotion or idea which cannot be expressed in any
other form. A fine statue is the core of a hundred poems, and
a fine poem is a score of symphonies; some music would need a
hundred paintings to substitute for it.[82] But this does not
support the theory that the better a work of art is the farther
it drifts away from other arts than its own; it merely stresses
the identity of individual emotion and of individual expression.
In fact a true work of art will bring our mind closer to all
branches of art, because it focuses our mind "on a given difini-
tion of form, or rhythm, so intensely that it becomes not only

[79]   "The Serious Artist", *Pavannes and Divisions*, 231.
[80]   "Camoens", *The Spirit of Romance*, 222.
[81]   "The Serious Artist", *Pavannes and Divisions*, 231.
[82]   *Gaudier Brzeska*, 96-97.

more aware of that given form, but more sensitive to all other forms, rhythms, defined planes, or masses". There is also another sort of art which aims at the unification of all arts. This kind of art, which may be called the Wagnerian, attempts to "confuse the spectator by smacking as many of his senses as possible at every possible moment". When it is successful, the spectator will be all in excitement and "you may sell him a rubber doll or a new cake of glassmender during the hurly-burly".[83]

The relation of poetry to drama is essentially the same as that of poetry to prose: the language of poetry is more densely charged than that of drama. Obviously this is due to the fact that, while the medium of poetry is words alone, that of drama is action, people moving about on the stage and using words. Drama need not rely on the charge which can be put into words but can call on gesture and mimicry and "impersonation" for assistance. The poet depends solely on words; the playwright is at the mercy of his actors, who do a good half of the work. But from a broader point of view the difference lies only in the manner of presentation; between poetry and drama there is no essential difference in subject-matter. Or one may go as far as to say that even the techniques of poetry and drama (together with some other arts and non-arts) are the same; both attempt to hold the audience's attention through expectation, suspense or surprise – even rhyme, a purely poetic device, is in the final analysis a scheme to arouse expectation. The poet should not accuse the dramatist of his "trickery", since the means of poetry is trickery, too.[84]

Pound has been quite fair to the playwright so far, and he largely remains so in all he has written for publication. But in private letters he seems unable to conceal his partiality for poetry over drama, and this is slightly reflected in his essays, too. He writes, for example:

I think the reason I loathe all stage stuff is that it is split. I can stand quite bad theatre *in* the theatre, but when I read Shxpr I

[83] "George Antheil", *Antheil and the Treatise on Harmony*, 32-33.
[84] "The Quality of Lope de Vega", *The Spirit of Romance*, 179-180.

don't think of stage, I think of people. Anything that asks the reader to think of effect or how it wd be on stage distracts from reality of fact presented. Even if it does appeal to the ballet russe or charlotte russe instincts of the bee-holder. Means the author not obsessed with reality of his subject.[85]

This leads him to say, for example, that the dramatist usually relapses into inferior poetry or neglects it altogether.[86] He also says, although with the proviso "as reading matter", that the Greek dramatists are not up to Homer, and that even Aeschylus is rhetorical.[87] At one time Pound seems to give silent consent to an Elizabethan specialist's suggestion that "Shakespeare, disgusted with his efforts or at least despairing of success, as a poet, took to the stage".[88]

Pound's preference of poetry to drama is partly due to his mistrust of public taste in art. His low estimate of the general public in understanding a work of art at times causes in him impatience, disgust, and even hatred. "The taste of the public is bad", he can make such a blunt statement. "The taste of the public is always bad."[89] When he is in a better mood, however, he is quite willing to undertake the job of being a teacher of literature, as he does in *How to Read* or *ABC of Reading*. At the root of the matter lies his belief that literary criticism is always technical, too technical for laymen. A literary work is an expression of personal conviction; one may agree or disagree, but cannot refute the writer. Only when the writer's art is bad, one can throw him out of count on the grounds of his technique.[90] But only practising poets really know about poetic technique; how can those who do not or cannot write verse know about versification? The argument leads to Pound's famous dictum that good poets alone can be good critics of poetry just as auto-mechanics alone are qualified to speak on the mechanism of automobiles. He can make

---

[85]   Letter to Ronald Duncan, 1938. *Letters*, 306.
[86]   "The Quality of Lope de Vega", *The Spirit of Romance*, 180.
[87]   *The ABC of Reading*, 31.
[88]   "How to Read", *Polite Essays*, 176.
[89]   "Imaginary Letters", *Pavannes and Divigations*, 55-56.
[90]   *Patria Mia*, 77.

such sweeping commentary as: "THE VALUE of criticism in proportion to actual making, is less than one to one hundred."[91] Criticism is commentary on the means and not on the end. True appreciation of literature and art should focus on the end. And one may approach the heart of art by thinking "what the creator must perforce have felt and known before he got round to creating them".[92] Art, after all, is communication. Since language is not a perfect medium of communicating every human emotion, there always remains a residue, "something in the man which does not get into his work".[93] This is why "the man is always more worth knowing than his books are".[94] It is why a work of art is always more valuable than its criticism.

However, literary criticism may improve itself by using the very means of art; a work of criticism might itself become a work of art. This is the idea which underlies Pound's five types of criticism well-known for its eccentricity: "criticism by discussion", "criticism by translation", "criticism by exercise in the style of a given period", "criticism via music", and "criticism in new composition".[95] Of these only the first type falls within the realm of traditional criticism. All the other types attempt to become criticism of art by becoming works of art themselves; they are red-hot iron criticizing fire. Pound put all these into practice himself. Many of his critical essays, particularly those included in *Literary Essays*, are fine examples of "criticism by discussion". Instances of "criticism by translation" are numerous too: Pound's translation, collected in *Translations of Ezra Pound*, include those from Greek, Latin, French, Tuscan, Italian, Provençal, Chinese and Japanese. His translations of Arnaut Daniel and Cavalcanti, which he refers to as part of his study in verse-form, may be considered as his "exercise in the style of a given period". Some poems in *Personae*, such as "Marvoil", "Sestina: Altaforte" and "Piere

[91]   "Aphorisms", *Pavannes and Divigations*, 231.
[92]   *Culture*, 114.
[93]   *Patria Mia*, 40.
[94]   *Ibid.*, 40.
[95]   "Date Line", *Make It New*, 4.

Vidal Old", are exercises, if they are exercises at all, in the style and subject-matter of Provençal poetry. Pound is also the composer of an opera "Villon", of which he says: "The music [in so far as the singing is intelligible] is ... a comment on, or an elucidation of, the form of the words and possibly of their meaning, or, if you like, of the emotive contents."[96] As for the last category, "criticism in new composition", Pound takes up T. S. Eliot's "Sweeney Agonistes" and "Seneca in Elizabethan Translation", and remarks that the poem is "infinitely more alive, more vigorous" than the essay.[97] Pound himself, in *Personae*, seems to be at least in part criticizing other poets and their works. The emotion embodied in "Homage to Sextus Propertius" are "defined largely, but not entirely, in Propertius' own terms".[98] *Hugh Selwyn Mauberley* is "an attempt to condense the James novel".[99] They are, in implication, a criticism of Propertius' or Henry James' writings.[100]

However, with all his emphasis on technical matters of poetry, with all his expositions and practice of five different types in literary criticism, Pound does not give us the impression of being an academic critic or a scholarly translator. He is, as we see him, rather a man leaning against his bookcase and talking about his favorite books, or a man very intent on educating the general public through art and literature. For him, in the end, literature does not exist in a vacuum, nor is it intended for a group of specialists alone. The function of literature, as he believes, is manifold and is closely related to the nature of literature. On the most elementary level literature corrects and improves language; it promotes the right use of words. And, since every thought or opinion is given its form through language and is conveyed to others through language, the clarity and vigor of every thought and opinion depend on the right use of words. Therefore, when this

---

[96]  *Guide to Kulchur*, 366.
[97]  "Date Line", *Make It New*, 4.
[98]  Letter to the Editor of the *English Journal*, 1931. *Letters*, 231.
[99]  Letter to Felix E. Schelling, 1922. *Letters*, 180.
[100]  Cf. Frederick Adler, *Ezra Pound and the Art of Poetry*.

medium goes rotten, when it becomes "slushy and inexact, or excessive or bloated", then "the whole machinery of social and of individual thought and order goes to pot".[101] "A nation", Pound reiterates, "which is slack in distinguishing the meaning of words, and which tolerates the use of ambiguous phrases, rots".[102]

On another level, literature is useful to society for the emotions and ideas which it embodies. These emotions and ideas are precious, since they are truer to reality, since they are spoken by those who are not afraid of social pressure. "If the poets don't make certain horrors appear horrible who will?" Pound asks. "Until the cells of humanity recognize certain things as excrement, they will stay in [the] human colon and poison it."[103] As there are in medicine the art of diagnosis and the art of cure, so in the arts there are the art of diagnosis and the art of cure – the cult of ugliness and the cult of beauty. People favor the cult of beauty; but the cult of ugliness, represented by such writers as Villon, Baudelaire, Corbière, Beardsley and Flaubert, is just as important. Satire, the most direct expression of it, is "surgery, insertions and amputations".[104] This function is inherent in art; it does not rely on the artist's conscious didactic intention. For this reason prerevolutionary authors in Russia usually leave the reader with "a conviction that there was something very wrong in Russia and that it needed alteration".[105] The artist, because of his deeper perception, is always too much ahead of any revolution, or reaction, or counter-reaction for his vote to have any immediate effect, and the statesmen of his time, as well as the general public, will not heed his words. But his prophecy will soon come true; the Russian Revolution, for one, bears its witness. "Artists", Pound declares, "are the antennae of the race".[106] An animal that neglects the warnings of its percep-

---

[101] "How to Read", *Polite Essays*, 164.
[102] "On Military Virtue", *Impact*, 251.
[103] Letter to Felix E. Schelling, 1922. *Letters*, 181.
[104] "The Serious Artist", *Pavannes and Divisions*, 225.
[105] "Open Letter to Tretyakov", *Impact*, 226.
[106] *The ABC of Reading*, 65.

tions will find it very hard to survive. "A nation which neglects the perceptions of its artist declines", Pound says. "After a while it ceases to act, and merely survives."[107] Perhaps people have vaguely felt the truth: the idea that the artist is insane has been fostered by the inferiority complex of the public.

Besides, the emotions and ideas which the true artist conveys are valuable because they are not mere "knowledge" but "understanding", the comprehension of human reality. Knowledge, while it is necessary and useful, is after all a set of catalogues of fixed concepts. But art teaches the process by which we approach knowledge. It opens one's eyes and lets one see the reality by oneself. Therefore, "once the process is understood it is quite likely that the knowledge will stay by a man, weightless, held without effort".[108] Furthermore, the opening of the eyes brings pleasure to man; art teaches and pleases, or pleases by teaching. A good literary work never bores one, because it relieves, refreshes and revives one's mind "with some form of ecstasy, by some splendor of thought, some presentation of sheer beauty, some lightning turn of phrase – laughter is no mean ecstasy".[109] It incites humanity to continue living; it eases the mind of strain and feeds it. Art functions as "nutrition of impulse".[110]

The dominant impression one gets in reading through Pound's voluminous writing is that of heterogeneity, a great variety of separate things co-existing with no apparent interrelation. Yet his ideas on poetry, when they are gathered together and seen from a viewpoint which transcends the historical or the topical, seem to show remarkable consistency. Pound was extremely sensitive to the limitations of individual man's faculties; he, therefore, always tried to broaden his perspective by learning other men's methods and approaches. Absolute truth did not exist, or was unknowable to man if it did; truth was a subjective thing lying in the perception of

---

[107]   *Ibid.*, 66.
[108]   *Culture*, 53.
[109]   "Praefatio ad Lectorem Electum", *The Spirit of Romance*, 80.
[110]   "How to Read", *Polite Essays*, 163.

each individual. The task of a poet was to present such "felt truth" by means of language. The subjects of poetry were as numerous as man's emotions and ideas, or their modifications, or their shades and shadows; they could be as lofty as God or Immortality, or as simple as a pine tree which looks like an old Japanese suit of armor. No one could condemn a poem for its subject-matter as long as it is an honest expression of the poet's conviction. The only objective criterion of literary criticism is the degree of precision with which the poet expresses his emotion, his "felt truth". Poetic technique should be the poet's central concern when he composes a poem; it is only through technique that he can make an accurate report of his emotion. The poet will have to distinguish carefully among different "primary emotions" and to adopt proper poetic forms accordingly. If the primary emotion is musical, he will compose a lyric poem; if pictorial, an imagist poem; if verbal, a poem of irony. The primary emotion, and not the poet's will, determines the poetic form; in this sense all good poems are objective, impersonal – "scientific". The value of poetry is ultimately the same as that of science; both provide accurate data on the condition of man, the former internal and the latter external. Or, for that matter, the function of poetry is the same as that of any other branch of human knowledge – history, economics, world politics, among others. Perhaps such divisions do not even exist in Pound's concept of knowledge; to him poetry is didactic, just as history and economics and political science are didactic. There are different kinds of truths as there are different areas of human knowledge. To express them with maximum precision one has to employ different kinds of languages, different kinds of approaches. Pound felt the need and did so.

# CHAPTER V

# TOWARD A DEFINITION OF POETRY

The preceding chapters have briefly outlined four writers' views on art and poetry. The views are diverse indeed: even between such close friends as Yeats and Pound there seems to be considerable difference in their ideas on verse-writing. The fact should surprise no one: rather, it would be amazing if one found many points of similarity between the two writers as remote as Zeami and Pound. Nevertheless, one will not fail to recognize, beneath the difference in methodology and terminology, certain fundamental ideas pointing toward a definition of poetry, a definition which is not confined to one country, one age, or one cultural tradition alone. To clarify these basic ideas, it will be convenient to focus our discussion upon a series of issues essential to any poetics: (1) life and art, (2) poetry and ideas (poetry, science and philosophy), (3) poetry and other arts, (4) the creative process, (5) the "mode of existence" of the poem, (6) the technique of poetry, and (7) the function of poetry.

Most theories concerning the relation of art to nature, or objective reality, may be placed somewhere between the two poles of naturalism and expressionism. At one pole stands the idea that literature should make an exact copy of actual happenings in life; at the other is the notion that a work of art is an expression of the artist's internal soul and has little to do with external reality. Ezra Pound certainly comes close to the former pole when he says that the artist must be a scientist in making an exact report on his observations. Zeami, from a dramatist's and actor's point of view, naturally makes imitation the most fundamental principle of his aesthetics: the artist, as he thinks, has a colorless soul which mirrors the universe. Bashō goes further and attempts the dissolution of any personal element in poetry. Even the "subjective" poet Yeats had to admit that "perhaps there is always some imitation" in art when his father, J. B. Yeats, wrote to him that all art was imitation of something in the outer world.[1] A pure expressionist theory which insists on the detachment of art from outside reality will be inadequate as long as literature takes its material from life and uses language for its medium.

The question of why and how art differs from nature is more complex. One of the simplest answers is given by pragmatic theories of art: any work of art tries to make a certain impression upon the audience and therefore chooses only those materials which fit the purpose. A classical example is that of Poe: the artist, as he believes, is concerned only with the Rhythmical Creation of Beauty and strives toward that sole aim. Zeami, in a subtler way, expresses the same view; in fact almost the whole of his writing on the art of the *nō* is concerned with the technique by which the performer may create certain artistic effects on the audience. In Zeami's way of thinking the nature of the emotional impact is the primary criterion of a work of art. He, therefore, talks about the "density" of imitation: an actor may imitate the speech and deportment of a graceful court lady as they are, while he may not do so in acting out a rustic woodcutter's role. Thus according to Zeami art is not a faithful reproduction of all aspects of life; it imitates only that part of life which produces a particular sensuous impression such as *yugen* or "the sublime". Both Yeats and Pound seem to have held a similar view when they were young. In a letter to a friend in 1900 Yeats remarks that the primary concern of poetry is to produce beauty whereas that of prose is to expound ideas.[2] Pound, in a letter to W. C. Williams in 1908, includes beauty in what he considers as the

[1]  Letter to J. B. Yeats, 1916. *Letters*, 607.
[2]  Letter to George Russell, 1900. *Letters*, 243.

ultimate attainments of poetic creation.[3] Both poets, however, soon dropped this kind of theory and grew increasingly didactic in their later years.

The weakness of a view like Zeami's becomes clear when it is compared with Bashō's. Bashō indeed advocates such ideas as *sabi, shiori,* and "lightness" which denote certain poetic moods, but these moods are firmly grounded in certain attitudes toward life; they are not only aesthetic ideas but philosophical concepts. A work of art created for the sake of pure aesthetic emotion, a tone or atmosphere devoid of moral implication, will not be a great work of literature as long as literature remains something which interprets human life, which comments on human experience. This is the main reason why many *nō* plays are not good works of literature; they aim at graceful beauty and pay little attention to the fact that their themes are commonplace, trite, and sentimental. They are saved only by their non-literary elements such as singing, dancing and mimicry. In this sense they may be compared to Western opera or ballet in which music, rather than dramatic literature, constitutes its merit. As a type of dramatic literature they are obviously inferior to Greek or Elizabethan drama, because they depend upon many elements exterior to literature.

The inadequacy of the view that art imitates nature only in those aspects which produce certain preconceived effects upon the audience is most obvious in the works of Zeami's followers like Kanze Kojirō. Zeami himself, however, seems to have been partly aware of it, when he says that the *nō* performer should not be too intent on creating the effect of elegant beauty. Then he goes on to say that an artist should not imitate the details of appearance but represent the "true intent". Here is the origin of the classical theories of art: the artist imitates "higher reality" or "the universal", rather than "everyday reality" or "the particular". The view presupposes an idealist notion of two worlds, the one which we live in, and the other which we live by. Yeats shares this view: he conceives the

[3] Letter to William C. Williams, 1908. *Letters*, 6.

world of imagination as against that of the senses, considering the first as eternal and the second as temporary. Man is, we have heard him say, "an artifice, an emphasis, an uncompleted arc perhaps". Yeats seems to have derived the idea from the Western idealist tradition, both Hellenist and Hebraic, but Zeami evidently borrowed it from Buddhism, very possibly from the esoteric Shingon school. Buddhist philosophy also assumes the existence of the two worlds, eternal and transient; man, with his limited senses, can get a glimpse of the eternal world only through the things of this world at some brief moments. The artist, as well as the monk, is a seer who can perceive the world invisible to ordinary eyes. Bashō, inheriting the same tradition, perhaps had a similar idea when he said: "To compose *haiku* is to treat reality while being in illusion."[4]

This comment by Bashō leads to the argument as to whether a fact presented in a literary work is true or false. The argument is an agelong one, starting with Plato in the West and with *The Tale of Genji*[5] in Japan. Bashō makes a flat statement elsewhere: "The art of poetry lies simply in a skillful way of telling a lie".[6] In a playful way he is challenging those who think that literature must present empirical facts as they are. To Bashō a "lie" means non-conformity to actual happenings in daily life; it is the opposite of "fact", not of "truth"; a "lie" may be truer than a "fact". Zeami and Yeats, being more ardent believers in the "other world," more positively insist on this point. In Zeami's view the highest type of beauty is created out of supreme truth far above everyday reality; "in Silla", we have heard him say, "the sun shines brightly at midnight". In Yeats's view a miracle is a form of revelation; in human history angels and devils are as important as kings and soldiers. Yeats believes, and Zeami seems to believe, that the true artist presents life not as it is but as it ought to be. Art imitates nature; but, since the picture of

[4]    Shikō, *Chinjō no hyō, SH*, 606.
[5]    Cf. Lady Murasaki, *A Wreath of Cloud*, 253-257.
[6]    Shikō, *Nijūgo-ka-jō, SH*, 38.

nature which an ordinary man holds is only a superficial and incomplete one, the artist creates a more nearly perfect picture of nature out of his own vision.

Here it may seem that the mimetic theory is approaching the expressive theory, because the fact that the artist imitates his vision of nature implies the self-expression of the artist. But those who advocate impersonal art, like Zeami, Bashō and Yeats, assume that there are really two selves in each person: the one which man is conscious of, and the other which is subconscious. The supporters of impersonal poetry invariably prefer the second self to the first, because the second self is "impersonal" in the sense that it is beyond man's control and belongs to the universe. In Yeats's terminology the dualism is between the self and the anti-self, between the individual memory and the Great Memory; he, of course, chooses the latter as the source of poetic inspiration and advises poets to suspend their desire and will so that images and symbols can generate by themselves. A similar idea is expressed by Zeami when he speaks of an actor who has no will to imitate. Bashō also seems to share the view when he says that the poet does not "make" a poem but something in him "becomes" a poem. In fact he carries the principle still further: he renounces the ego not only in poetry but in life also. For him it is not enough that art imitates nature; life itself should become art.

The question, however, remains as to the objectivity of "higher reality" or "the impersonal self". To assume the existence of such reality or self is itself a subjective judgement. The concept of "higher reality" or "the impersonal self" differs from person to person. Ezra Pound, therefore, legitimately has doubts about the existence of absolute truth and abstains from speaking of God, eternity or the soul in any definite terms. He believes that the artist can imitate nature only when his mind gets a hold on nature or part of nature; imitation is inevitably interpretation. But if one assumes this "interpreted reality" or "felt truth" as something external to one's ego, an accurate reproduction of such reality or truth without the intervention of the poet's own desire or will may be said to be "impersonal" art. A poet, as Pound thinks, would let the "interpreted reality" or "felt truth" transform itself into a poem, himself being a mere catalyzer which accelerates the transformation; the poem, thus made, is "impersonal".

When Pound's view is carried a little further toward subjectivism, there are formed various expressive theories. As a matter of fact Pound himself has partly subscribed to an expressive theory. Art, we have heard him say, is "an emphasis, a segregation" of some component of the "universal intelligence" for the purpose of making it more perceptible. There are some artists who put emphasis on certain components according to their philosophical beliefs; they are "philosophical" artists, as against "mediumistic" artists who can exist only through their art. To "philosophical" poets poetry becomes only a means of self-expression, if by "self" we mean one's internal reality, the whole range of one's awareness. In this type of poets poetry expresses their private philosophy – not necessarily systematic ideas but any emotions or ideas, any shades or fragments of emotions or ideas pertinent to human experience. At one time Pound carries this view to an extreme and even makes self-expression a criterion of greatness by saying that the poet's merit depends on his capacity "to dispense with external subjects altogether, to create from himself or from elements".

The mimetic and expressive theories of art are not mutually antithetical but different only in emphasis. The mimetic theory would maintain that the artist is a "mirror" which reflects nature, that he tries to minimize personal elements in art so that his work may contain maximum external reality. Yet the concept of nature or external reality varies among different men; "objectivity" or "universality" itself relies on the personal judgement of each individual. Thus Yeats, admittedly a "mediumistic" poet, sings out his personal emotions and ideas in a most personal style. Zeami, who holds that the ideal artist has a "transparent" soul, writes nō plays which reveal a clearly defined attitude toward life – that of a Buddhist. Even in the case of Bashō, who consistently renounces personal elements in poetry, the very negation of individual personality is an expression of the poet's self, since it presumes his "aesthetic", "unhuman" or "bystander's" attitude toward life. Here arises the expressive theory of art which maintains that the artist is a "lamp" which shines with or without light from outside, that he puts forth his personal emotions and ideas through his work. One cannot, however, think of the artist's soul in isolation; it is nourished, conditioned and expressed through external reality – the tradition and environment; its very essence is the "elements" without which its existence itself might be doubted. If the artist is to express his soul by means of art, he can do so only by defining it in terms of the things external to it. The one says art is an imitation of nature; the other says it is an expression of the artist's soul. But an imitation of nature can be done only through the artist's soul, and an expression of the artist's soul only through natural objects. Mimetic and expressive theories merge into one another in maintaining that art tries to represent reality; they differ only in the interpretation of reality. The ultimate difference between the two theories lies outside the realm of poetics; it lies in philosophy, in the way a person creates his vision of life.

But, whatever interpretation one may make of reality, one must in some way or another resolve the dualism of the soul and the universe before one frames and moulds reality into poetry. Any great artist or philosopher probes deep into the relation between man and the cosmos and attempts to illuminate it. A great work of art arises out of such an attempt, and the impact one feels at its presence comes from such a perception of ultimate reality. What is this impact like? It varies, of course, from work to work, from writer to writer. In Zeami it is *yūgen* first, and "the sublime" later. A feeling which pervades the two is the sense of life's transience in its most elevated form. Man, set against the universe, is tiny, fragile and insignificant; he should submit himself to the great being without struggle. The feeling of *yūgen* arises when man, awakening to this fact, sadly submits himself. The feeling of "the sublime" appears when he does this with calm and serenity, without sadness. To some extent Bashō takes over the idea of "the sublime", too. The feeling of *sabi* is produced when man accepts the tortures of living with peace of mind. When man does this with a smile, there emerges "lightness". Zeami and Bashō resolve the dualism of man and the universe by making man completely surrender to the universe. Perhaps the term "surrender" is not adequate, since neither Zeami nor Bashō recognizes a struggle between man and the cosmos; he sees the former as part of the latter. Such a resolution, however, is difficult in the Romantic tradition of Western culture, in which an objective mode of perception developed very early in history. The ego is not to be destroyed but to be developed to the full; the universe is not to be revered but to be fought with; one should rage and rage before going into the darkness of the night. In Yeats's view, therefore, personal emotions like joy, grief, love and jealousy are not to be suppressed but to be intensified to such a great degree that they become pure and aimless. The tension coming out of a struggle between opposites is the very essence of human vitality. The impact arising from such tension is that of tragedy. In Zeami's and Bashō's poetics there is no possibility of tragedy, since it allows no possibility of man's fight against the power of the universe; in Yeats's concept of poetry tragic tension occupies the central place. Pound is different: he tries to resolve the dualism of man and the universe neither by making the former surrender to the latter, nor by uniting the two in a tragic tension, but by leaving the two as they are and seeing the connection, wherever possible, in each individual case.

However, all branches of human learning are primarily a search for truth; science and philosophy are particularly concerned with man's place in the universe. Poetry differs from these in its conception of truth and its approach toward the conception. The difference between poetry and science is noted by Pound on its most elementary level: it lies in subject-matter. Science treats the external world; when it deals with man, it sees him in terms of physical and biological components which constitute his body. The sole concern of poetry is man, the human mind. To Pound, therefore, the prime feature of poetry exists in its capacity to search into such a complex and elusive subject as the human mind; the method is something which is necessitated by the nature of its subject-matter. To Yeats, on the other hand, the methodology is of prime importance, for, as he thinks, the method of science is incapable of discovering truth. The scientific method, built on observation, analysis and reasoning, always focuses on parts, and not on the whole, of a living organism; it merely tears apart a living creature; it never creates a new life. Hence emerges Yeats's hatred of science, and his yearning for the Middle Ages, for the world of myths and legends, and for the Oriental way of life. Indeed Zeami's and Bashō's modes in approaching truth are anti-scientific. Zeami recognizes the highest reality in a super-scientific sphere, where a black peak stands solitarily among snow-covered mountains, or where the sun shines brightly at midnight. Bashō advises one to enter the life of a natural object rather than to examine it objectively; an object should be seen from the inside rather than from the outside, in its totality rather than in its parts which build up the whole. Zeami and Bashō cannot think of a natural object in isolation from the self which perceives it; an objective fact does not exist, or, if it does, it exists only at the bottom of a great chain of being.

However, to pass this sort of evaluative judgement on science and poetry in terms of methodology may be misleading. The aims of science and poetry differ, hence the difference in method, as Pound rightly notes. Both science and poetry aim at the discovery of truth, indeed; but the nature of truth differs in science and in poetry. In science a proposition is valid when it exactly corresponds to objective facts. But in poetry anything can be valid as long as it corresponds to man's thought or emotion. Science deals with empirical truth, poetry with speculative truth: the method of science is observation and analysis to attain the former kind of truth, and that of poetry is intuition and assimilation to reach for the latter.

The choice between the two kinds of truth is a matter of personal preference. Zeami and Bashō inadvertently, and Yeats deliberately, choose the latter; they have to, so long as they remain poets.

In this respect philosophy is closer to poetry, since it also takes human mind for its subject-matter and is concerned with assumed, rather than verifiable, truth. But it differs from poetry in that it is a system of abstract generalizations. Generalization presupposes, and consequently exaggerates, the similarity between man and man, between objects in nature. In actual life no two things are identical, as Yeats remarks; generalization is removed from life as it deduces certain common parts from many unidentical things. When these generalizations are collected and made into a system, the system will be still further removed from actual life. Yeats and Pound do not like abstract philosophy for this reason. Poetry brings philosophical ideas close to life by giving a concrete form to them, by weaving them into a living story. Poetry is more particular than philosophy because it circumscribes a situation in which a certain generalization is true. Poetry is more ambiguous than philosophy because it picks up only one possibility out of many and leaves the others unsaid. It is particular as individual man's life is particular; it is ambiguous as life can be lived on many different levels.

Yeats and Pound renounce abstract philosophy, but not philosophical ideas or attitudes. In fact Yeats remarks, quoting from Goethe: "'A poet needs all philosophy, but he must keep it out of his work', though that is not always necessary."[7] Pound says: "A work of art need not contain any statement of a political or of a social or of a philosophical conviction, but it nearly always implies one."[8] The themes of poetry are the themes of philosophy also; both take their materials out of human experience, external and internal. Poetry is philosophical in the sense that it always expresses a certain attitude or attitudes toward life. Perhaps this is an important point:

[7]   "The Symbolism of Poetry", *Essays*, 189.
[8]   *Patria Mia*, 77.

ideas implied in poetry are philosophical but not necessarily philosophy – they are adjectival but not necessarily substantive. The evil of abstract philosophy is in its attempt to force the philosophical into philosophy. A certain type of poet, Pound's "philosophical" type, does the reverse: he transforms "philosophy" into "poetry with philosophical attitudes". Of course there is the other type, the "mediumistic"; the poets of this type create their work directly out of life, without the process of abstraction into a system. Zeami and Bashō belong to the latter type.

The points at which poetry differs from science and systematic philosophy are the points at which it approaches music and the plastic arts. The common bond among different arts has been recognized from various angles – chiefly from two standpoints: the reader's or spectator's, and the artist's. All arts are united, first, in that they aim at the creation of beauty rather than a didactic or practical goal, and secondly, in that they are by and large the product of emotion and intuition instead of intellect and logic. The first point is stressed by Zeami, who believes that the effect of *yūgen* or "the sublime" can be attained only through a perfect union of music and drama: "singing and acting are originally two different things", he says, "but those who have accomplished their art to the point where the two become one can be said to be supreme artists."[9] As we have seen, the *nō* itself is a composite art, mingling the elements of poetry, drama, music, dancing, painting and sculpture. This idea, of course, is nothing new in the West: the masque, opera, and ballet are some of its examples. Even in the case of a clearly single art one often says such things as a certain poem having the effect of music or a certain musical composition giving the impression of painting. One is recognizing the oneness of different arts in terms of artistic effect.

Yet poetry is still more significantly related to other arts in terms of its creative process. Unlike science and philosophy, poetry is not the product of pure reason, and in this it has

[9]   *Fūshi kaden, ZJH*, I, 112-113.

much in common with other arts. One might assume some sort of spirit, intuitive and creative, permeating all arts; one may call it "the poetic sentiment" as Poe does, or "the poetic spirit" as Bashō does. "The Poetic Sentiment", says Poe, "may develop itself in various modes – in Painting, in Sculpture, in Architecture, in the Dance – very especially in Music."[10] "There is one common element", says Bashō, "which permeates Saigyō's *waka*, Sōgi's linked verse, Sesshū's painting, and Rikyū's tea ceremony. It is a poetic spirit ..." Yeats thinks of this spirit as the ideal of man's life, saying: "As this ideal is rediscovered, the arts, music and poetry, painting and literature, will draw together." Pound conceives two types of poetry: the one, "a sort of poetry where music, sheer melody, seems as if it were just bursting into speech", and the other, "another sort of poetry where painting or sculpture seems as if it were 'just coming over into speech'".[11] The question as to precisely what this spirit is has caused different responses among artists; but one common bond is that it is not abstract, not of pure intellect – it is intuitive, irrational, mystical. The Romantic tradition strongly emphasized this point: reason is a principle of analysis and dissociation – it cannot create. Intuition is creative, as it is the principle of assimilation and integrity, as it discovers relationship between disparate objects and transforms them into a unity. This creative spirit, giving energy to a work, becomes a distinguishing mark of the arts. Pound compares the energy to a flowing stream and aptly says that the scientist is concerned with the banks and riverbed, whereas the artist's concern is with that which flows. Science and philosophy do not have this energy; poetry, fine arts and music do.[12]

The difference between science and poetry has been discussed time and again by a number of people, because there has been an ever-growing strife between the two since the rise of science in modern life. The difference among the arts has

[10] "The Poetic Principle", *The Great Critics*, 590.
[11] *Gaudier Brzeska*, 95.
[12] "Praefatio ad Lectorem Electum", *The Spirit of Romance*, 7-8.

far less frequently been examined, partly because there has been no such strife. The question nevertheless exists as to what differentiates poetry from other arts. An obvious answer is that while music and the plastic arts work with sound and plane respectively, the poet uses language for his material; the difference lies in the medium of expression or representation. This, however, does not answer the question how a particular person comes to choose a particular medium. Yeats at one time thought that poetry was most nearly perfect when it was nearest the condition of music; why, then, did he not compose music? His answer was that he was by nature not musically minded. Bashō's theory of communion with nature may be fully realized through painting too; why, then, did he not paint? He actually did, but he said he had not been trained in painting and started learning it under one of his disciples. These facts seem to point toward a rather commonplace observation: the artist chooses his art by natural gift or training. The poet is a person who, either by nature or by training, perceives things poetically; the musician, for the same reason, sees happenings in life in musical terms. Or, if one is reluctant to have recourse to such elusive things as natural gift or training, one may hold a view that a person can think and feel only by the help of some medium. Some men are inclined to think and feel in terms of picture; others, in terms of sound; still others, in terms of plane. Or one may maintain a theory, as Pound does, that it is not the person but the thought or feeling itself which determines the medium. At one time a certain person thinks by making use of image since visualization is the most suitable mode of thinking at that moment. But at another time the same person may meditate through sound, if the contents of the meditation are of auditory nature. This "primary pigment" of thought or emotion determines the mode of expression: if the primary pigment is musical, the person will compose music or musical poetry; if verbal, literature. This theory of Pound's, while very interesting, is still vague as to what determines the nature of the "primary pigment". Is it the outward stimulant? The structure of the person's mentality? The person's will? Or the combination of these factors? Pound gives no answer. But perhaps these questions are beyond the realm of poetics; they belong to psychology. As far as poetics is concerned this much is true: an emotion or idea is conceived through a certain medium and is most effectively expressed through that medium. This medium is what differentiates one art from another.

Poetry, then, unlike science and philosophy and like music and the plastic arts, springs primarily from the poet's sub-conscious – what T. S. Eliot calls "pre-logical mentality". Such mentality runs counter to that part of man's mind which controls his ordinary activities, the conscious, and therefore often contradicts the manners and practice set up by tradition and society. The artist, thus, is "possessed" or "insane". The sympathizers of art, of course, would not like the latter term; Pound thinks the idea of the artist's being insane roots in the general public's inferiority complex. They would rather say the artist is "divinely possessed" – he is inspired by the Muse, or, in Yeats's term, by the Divine Purpose. The question is the one which we have already discussed: what is reality? To a scientist like Freud ultimate reality is empirical reality, and the poet, obsessed with his unfulfilled desires, dreams a dream which tries to compensate for the frustration. To a poet like Yeats, on the other hand, it is a dream which is ultimate reali-ty; reality lies in the collective unconscious, in the Great Memory. However, putting aside all these evaluative judge-ments, one cannot deny that the act of artistic creation is sub-conscious in its beginning. Zeami conceives of "the bone", or "pre-art", in contrast with "the flesh" and "the skin", as the most essential of artistic creation. Also when he talks of the artist's soul being the vessel of the universe in the vast windless way of emptiness, he seems to approach Yeats's description of the creative process in which the artist suspends critical faculty as well as desire and lets various images pass before the mind's eye. Yeats's notion that the artist's soul "passes into a slight trance" at the moments of creativity is essentially the same as Bashō's idea of "inspiration", "a flash of insight into an object".

All this may be explained by Pound's remark that the artist works with the "primary emotion", the prototype of emotion before it comes up to his consciousness. As soon as the "primary emotions" come up to one's consciousness, one's ego will start functioning and try to generalize, abstract and harden them. The poet's mode of perception is mystic; it is, in Pound's term, "a sudden outspurt of mind which takes the form demanded by the problem".

The poet, however, distinctly differs from a mere day-dreamer or a lunatic in that he has a perfect control over his vision. Freud distinguishes the poet from the madman by the former's capacity to return from the dreamland. Pound notes that the poet is able to detach himself from his dream and to make a precise report of it, which the lunatic cannot do. Yeats even tried to control his dreaming: for instance, he put certain flowers and leaves upon his pillow or bedside so that he might have a "vision", a coherent dream, during his sleep.[13] Bashō, from a slightly different angle, teaches the importance of self-control upon facing a very moving spectacle. Dohō records:

The Master said: "When one faces a landscape of supreme beauty, one is carried away by emotions and is unable to compose a poem. When one observes something, one should keep it alive in memory, copy it down in prose, and then compose a poem out of it in tranquility. One should be cautious not to be carried away by emotions. If one has too many things coming up into one's mind and is unable to compose a poem, one should make a note of them."[14]

That which controls dreams, emotions and ideas is art. Hence Pound's emphasis on artistic technique, Yeats's on the *coherent* dream and myth, and perhaps Bashō's self-confinement to the seventeen-syllable poetic form, and Zeami's elaborate curriculum for the actor's training. The artist needs to be a fanciful day-dreamer on the one hand, and a strictly disciplined crafts-man on the other. The separation of the technician from the dreamer may become a basis for the evaluation of a work of art. "The more perfect the artist", says Eliot for example, "the

[13]  "Anima Mundi", *Essays*, 509.
[14]  *Sanzōshi, SH*, 182.

more completely separate in him will be the man who suffers and the mind which creates; the more perfectly will the mind digest and transmute the passions which are its material."[15]

Here arises the controversial question as to whether or not the emotion felt by the poet and that embodied in the poem are the same, and whether or not the emotion embodied in the poem and that felt by the reader are the same. The question is an extremely important one, since it virtually decides the "mode of existence" of the poem, leading to the basic principle of literary criticism. The majority of literary scholars in the past seem to have thought that the poem is identical with the poet's original experience, and that to read the poem is to go through that experience. *Paradise Lost*, for instance, presents Milton's state of mind at a certain time of his career; to study the epic, therefore, is to illuminate that state of mind. The theory, however, can be easily refuted by referring to the poet's creative process, as suggested, for example, in the passages of Bashō and Eliot cited above. Actually the core of Bashō's poetics consists in the idea that the poet transforms the original emotion (like loneliness or pity) into the "aesthetic emotion" (like *sabi* or *shiori*). According to Bashō the emotion felt by the poet and that embodied in the poem are distinctly different: the former is the "personal emotion", and the latter the "impersonal mood". The same is true in Eliot's notion: the former is the "emotion", the latter the "feelings", and the poem the "objective correlative". Pound also admits the difference: the poet is never able to reproduce his original emotion; at best the reproduction is "the nearest equation that he was capable of putting into words". The poet's original emotion is never completely realized in the poem, since the creative process is not a mechanical procedure of reproduction but a component of various factors simultaneously working – the poet's conscious and "unconscious" intention, the inadequacy of the language, the convention of the literary form, and so forth. The poem is the poet's original emotion transformed throught art.

[15] *Selected Essays, 1917-1932*, 7-8.

It is interesting, however, to observe that among those who do not question the disparity between original and aesthetic emotions there are contrary trends in the preference of these two emotions. Some, Bashō among them, rank the aesthetic emotion over the original emotion; others, like Yeats, reverse the evaluation. To Bashō the original and aesthetic emotions signify two states of the poet's mind; the one before, and the other after, the purification of the soul. By composing a *haiku* the poet purges his egotism; the poem, a result of the purgation, should therefore be preferred to the poet's original state of mind. In contrast with this attitude Yeats remarks:

Till one has expressed a thing it is like an untidy, unswept, undusted corner of a room. When it is expressed one feels cleaner, and more elegant, as it were, but less profound so I suppose something is lost in expression.[16]

Yeats recognizes the purifying effect of verse-writing, but then notes the loss of "something" in the process of composition. The loss occurs because the language is inadequate in expressing all the delicate shades of the poet's original emotion. Here Yeats seems to be moving toward Pound's dictum: "The man is always more worth knowing than his books are." In fact Yeats confesses that Coleridge delights him more as man than as poet, and that this is because Coleridge had "some kind of illumination which was, as always, only in part communicable".[17]

One might be able to reconcile, at least in part, these two opposing views by admitting the limitation in the expressive capacity of art. The emotion embodied in a good work of art is "higher" than ordinary emotions in the sense that it is not available in ordinary life where man is bound by social, moral and biological factors. The aesthetic emotion is enriched by the poet's imagination which is over and above these restrictions. Yet one may assume such "aesthetic emotion" in the poet's mind as he creates a poem. This hypothetical "aesthetic

[16]    Letter to J. B. Yeats, 1917. *Letters*, 627.
[17]    *Pages from a Diary*, 12-13.

emotion" would be "higher" than its counterpart in the actual poem, because the poem suffers the restrictions of the language and artistic convention. But by assuming such an emotion one risks a grave danger. This ideal, unexpressed and inexpressible "aesthetic emotion" in the poet's mind, is a subjective, elusive thing, indeed; it is inaccessible, even to the poet himself, after the moments of creation.

The root of the matter lies in the question of "mode of existence". Where does a poem exist? – in the poet's mind, in the reader's mind, in the text of the poem, or elsewhere? Pound gives a clear-cut answer: "how to see works of art? Think what the creator must perforce have felt and known before he got round to creating them." Pound still holds the idea that technique of poetry is always imperfect, and so he refers the reader back to the "aesthetic emotion" in the poet's mind. The reader, however, must approach that ideal state of mind through the poem itself, and not through the poet's letters or other writings outside of the poem. Pound is quite clear about this: he even declares that bad critics are easily distinguished from good ones because they always discuss the poet and not the poem.[18] In Pound's opinion, then, the poem exists in the poet's mind, in a certain state of mind in him of which the actual poem is an imperfect replica. The experience which the reader goes through upon reading a poem is three times removed from the poet's original experience. The reader's emotion is only a "weaker copy" of the original. Yeats had a similar view, particularly when he was young. Once he even held a view that general readers could never completely understand his work since he alone had the private "key" to his symbolism. He gave only the surface story to the reader and kept the real poem to himself.

Zeami, although he is never explicit on this matter, seems to believe that a work of art lies in the spectator's mind. Obviously the *nō* play does not lie in its text; the *nō* is complete only when it is performed on the stage, with its recitation, music and dancing. It exists only partly in the mind of the

[18]    *The ABC of Reading*, 68-69.

writer, who has to rely heavily on the actors and musicians for the full effect of his work. The *nō* writer would never think of writing a play for himself as Yeats did in writing stories and essays; the *nō* does not exist without its audience. Such a theory is very fragile in that it has to rely on the response of the audience. It gets into immediate difficulty when it copes with the audience of different taste. In fact Zeami admits that it is impossible for a *nō* performance to gain the admiration of all the spectators in the theater.[19] I. A. Richards has tried to escape from this difficulty by assuming a hypothetical "ideal reader". Zeami, fortunately, had a most refined and sophisticated group of people for his audience. He once said that in the capital the audience was so good at evaluating and criticizing the *nō* that the performer, aware of the criticism or not, could in time attain a high stage of artistic achievement.[20] One may say that his was a rare case in which the actual audience came remarkably close to the "ideal audience". According to Zeami, then, the play exists in the audience's mind, but the audience is almost the "ideal audience"; here Zeami's idea is similar to Richards'. Pound and Yeats maintain that the true poem is the actual written poem plus all its original ingredients which remain unexpressed in the poet's mind. Zeami seems to believe that the true work of art is the actual concrete work plus all its extraneous effects which are pressed upon the audience's mind. In either case a work of art consists in the actual physical existence of the work plus *x*, some qualities unstated but potential in the author or in the work. Both theories contain the danger of falling into relativism in interpreting a work of art.

Bashō's position is somewhat different from either, and seemingly incoherent. On the one hand he believes that the author's inspired moment is everything: the written text of the poem is nothing more than a scrap of paper. If one can be in the *haiku* mood, one does not even have to compose a poem. On the other hand there are numerous instances in

[19]  *Hana no kagami*, ZJH, I, 389.
[20]  *Ibid.*, 369-370.

which Bashō "corrected" his disciples' poems, and often for a
reason which seems to have little to do with the inspired
moments of the original author. We have already seen the
case where he changed the line "In the dense pine-wood" to
"It is hailing". If a poem is the product of the poet's personal
experience, how can someone else correct or improve the
poem? Bashō goes even further in a well-known anecdote
concerning Kyorai's *haiku*:

> On the rocky cliff...
> Here, too, is the guest
> of the moon.

Bashō asked Kyorai who "the guest of the moon" was. Kyorai
answered it was a stranger. Bashō then said: "How much
more interesting it will be if you call yourself the guest of the
moon."[21] The anecdote has puzzled many a scholar of Japanese literature. The original author, who has all the circum-
stantial facts about the composition of the poem, is explicating
the meaning; nevertheless Bashō makes up a different interpretation by himself and even imposes it upon the original
author of the poem. Bashō, we may say then, seems to believe
that a poem can be an autonomous entity, that it does not
necessarily demand of the reader to adhere to every detail of
the author's conscious intention, and, therefore, that a well-
trained critic might be able to improve upon the poem with his
own interpretation of the circumstances under which the
poem was made. Instead of assuming an ideal "aesthetic
emotion" in the author's mind, Bashō tries to attain the best
interpretation possibly drawn from the poem, irrespective
of the author's intended meaning. Bashō differs from Zeami
too in that he sees the true poem within the actual existence of
the poem, not in the effect of the poem. Whereas Pound,
Yeats and Zeami admit some extrinsic elements into the final
meaning of the poem, Bashō excludes all these and conceives
the poem to be a self-contained whole. Of course, doubt

[21]   *Kyorai shō, SH*, 247.

remains as to what the best interpretation is. Bashō would answer that the criterion is the degree to which his principles of *sabi*, *shiori*, "lightness", etc. are realized in the poem. In the *haiku* just cited, for instance, Bashō's interpretation would bring out more of "lightness" than Kyorai's; therefore, the former explication is better than the latter. Bashō's theory would require utmost sensitivity on the interpreter's part; otherwise there will occur cases in which a poem is interpreted against its (not the author's) intention, or a poem of *sabi* is evaluated by the standard of "lightness". However, the idea that the true poem exists in the structure of the poem itself seems to be more adequate than any other on the question of "mode of existence".

Whether the ultimate existence of the poem lies in the author's or reader's mind or in the poem itself, the experience of creating or reading a poem may be said to be teleological: the author or reader recognizes that there is *the* meaning in the poem and strives to attain that meaning. Thus the question of poetic technique becomes very important, since technique is the instrument with which the poet or reader reaches for the final meaning of the poem. Those who deny that moral implications of poetry are basic to its evaluation go so far as to say that execution is the only criterion of poetic creation. Among the foremost elements of technique is the use of language; language to the poet is sound to the musician, color to the painter. Poetic language is distinguished from ordinary language by the fact that it is "elevated", "intensified", or "evocative".

One may give a definition of poetry in terms of its language. Poetry, says Pound, is simply language charged with meaning. "A poem", Yeats affirms, "is an elaboration of the rhythms of common speech and their association with profound feeling."[22] "The basic principle of composition", says Zeami, "is to convey meaning in the briefest words." Words in poetry, as the poet loads them with meaning, come to have not only denotative but highly connotative and emo-

[22] "Modern Poetry", *Essays, 1931-1936*, 28.

tive meaning. Each word is used in its greatest capacity; its sound and "feel" have far more significance in poetry than in common language. Therefore, says Pound, every word in a poem must have a reason for being there. "Do not use even a single syllable wastefully", reiterates Bashō, "since the *haiku* must be composed only in seventeen syllables".[23] One way of charging words with meaning is to use words which appear in the work of past poets, thereby invoking the reader's associations. "The secret of *nō* writing", Zeami teaches, "lies in the linking of various words and phrases used in classical poetry." In this method, however, there is the danger of the poem becoming commonplace or inviting stock response alone. Therefore Zeami makes a concession: "There are cases in which hard and uncommon words fit better."[24] Bashō, Yeats and Pound, born in the eras when there were too many "poetic" words, were far more keenly aware of the danger. "The essence of *haiku* composition", writes Bashō, "lies in the fresh use of the common language. It does not call for classical writers' words".[25] Bashō is referring to the contemporary *waka* and linked-verse writers whose poems were filled with sentimental, worn-out words of classical poetry. Likewise, Yeats and Pound were bewildered by the rhetoric of Victorian poetry, and they vigorously advocated the elimination of hackneyed vocabulary from the poetry of the new age. "Words are always getting conventionalized to some secondary meaning", writes Yeats. "It is one of the works of poetry to take the truants in custody and bring them back to their right senses. Poets are the policemen of language; they are always arresting those old reprobates the words."[26] A point in the imagist program was the cleansing of old exhausted vocabulary. Pound is quite persistent on this: "Objectivity and again objectivity, and expression: no hindside-beforeness, no straddled adjectives (as 'addled mosses dank'), no Tennysonianess of speech:

[23]  *Tabine-ron, SH,* 232.
[24]  *Fūshi kaden, ZJH,* I, 172-173.
[25]  *Kyō no mukashi.* Quoted in Okazaki, "Haikai to renga", *Kokubungaku kaishaku to kanshō,* XXV (1960), no. 5, 2.
[26]  Letter to Ellen O'Leary, 1889. *Letters,* 109-110.

nothing – nothing that you couldn't, in some circumstance, in the stress of some emotion, actually say". The reason for this is: "When one really feels and thinks, one stammers with simple speech."[27] Poetry must be a direct treatment of the "thing", whether subjective or objective; nothing extraneous should enter between the "thing" and its expression.

Another way of giving force to language is found in the use of rhythm. Poetic language develops its metrical and rhythmical functions to such a great extent that it at times comes close to the realm of music. A word, a phrase, or a sentence expands in complexity and intensity when its sound value is made to constitute an integral part of its meaning. Thus an emotion, strong or delicate, is best expressed in rhythmic language. Zeami takes a full advantage of this fact: every *nō* play consists of prose and verse passages, the former used generally in narrating a story or presenting a conversation, and the latter mainly in recording emotional utterance of a person in the play. When the monk describes his journey, he uses the regular rhythm of alternating five- and seven-syllable units. When the sinner narrates how he has been tormented in hell, he adopts a rhythm expressive of agony, with quickened tempo and without a regular syllabic pattern. Bashō wrote a good deal of *haibun*, a combination of prose and *haiku*. He used prose in describing his journey or an incident related to the journey, but relied on the *haiku* when he expressed certain states of mind he came to have at some particular moments on the journey. In Yeats's as well as in Pound's view rhythm was something which combined literature with music, as we have already seen. But these English poets were, just as in the case of poetic diction, very sensitive to the use of mellow, rhetorical, conventional poetic rhythm. Accordingly they stressed the importance of creating an individual rhythm. Yeats and Pound, however, seem to differ from each other in the way they have arrived at that conclusion. In Yeats's opinion rhythm is the poet's conscious arrangement of sound in order to invoke a certain emotion. It is part of the poet's

[27]    Letter to Harriet Monroe, 1915. *Letters*, 49.

ego, it belongs to him; therefore, "rhythm is not imitation".[28] But Pound believes in "absolute rhythm", a rhythm which exactly corresponds to the poet's emotion; rhythm, in other words, is inherent in the emotion itself and does not lie in the conscious will of the poet. Since every emotion is unique, every rhythm must be unique. In short, according to Yeats rhythm is created by the poet's conscious mind; its nature is determined by the individuality of the poet. According to Pound it is an offspring of the "primary emotion" within the poet's subconscious mind; its nature is determined by the individuality of the emotion. This difference of opinion perhaps in part explains the reason why Pound advocated *vers libre*, and why Yeats's poems, whether lyrical or dramatic, are all permeated with a highly individual rhythm.

While rhythm and meter appeal to the auditory imagination, image, metaphor and symbol appeal to the visual faculty in the main. These devices are particularly effective in poetry, since poetry attempts a representation of truth conceived through the senses. If poetry primarily seeks "emotional assent" rather than "verifiable truth", these devices become essential to its technique. Moreover, they are not simply devices of expression; they are means of meditation, instruments with which the poet formulates his thought. Perhaps we had better say they are thought itself, because any thought without them would be reduced to mere abstraction. Image, metaphor and symbol, as used in poetry, present thought in its complexity, with all its concomitant emotions and ideas.

How these three terms differ among themselves is a question practically impossible to answer. It may be generally assumed that an image is a visual (and in some cases, auditory) presentation of perception, that a metaphor is a presentation of one perception in terms of another, and that a symbol combines the functions of both an image and a metaphor. However, poets and scholars have used the terms interchangeably or in clearly different senses. Yeats recognizes the difference between the metaphor and the symbol: the symbol is more

[28]  Letter to J. B. Yeats, 1916. *Letters*, 608.

"profound" and "subtle", and therefore more "moving", than the metaphor.[29] He makes no noticeable distinction between the image and the symbol; he only uses the latter term much more frequently. In contrast, Pound is very fond of the term "image" and does not like the "symbol". While he does not seem to distinguish between the image and the metaphor, he emphatically differentiates the "symbol" from the image by its traditionally fixed value. But, aside from the question of terminology, it cannot be doubted that the "image" and the "symbol" occupy the central position in the poetics of Pound and Yeats respectively. The crucial question is the difference, if any, between Pound's "image" and Yeats's "symbol". Liberally interpreted, the two seem to be the same. Pound defines his "image" as "an intellectual and emotional complex" which gives "that sense of sudden liberation; that sense of freedom from time limits and space limits; that sense of sudden growth, which we experience in the presence of the greatest works of art". Yeats, referring to his "symbol", writes that the imaginative writer "identifies himself – to the neglect of his own soul, alas! – with the soul of the world, and frees himself from all that is impertinent in that soul, an ascetic not of women and wine, but of the newspapers". Both Pound and Yeats are thinking of a certain verbal unit which, by exerting a magical power upon the participant's senses, liberates him from the spiritual prison he has been confined to. Man is imprisoned in everyday life; his faculties, bound by social and moral codes, cannot attain their full development. Pound's "image" or Yeats's "symbol" unbinds man's imagination by freeing it from the ego, from the conscious mind, in an instant of time.

However, between Pound's "image" and Yeats's "symbol" there seems to lie a significant difference. Pound's "image" is inherent in the object; the object itself generates the image. According to Pound, the poet attains a certain perception, subjective or objective, which will form itself into the "primary emotion"; if the emotion is of visual kind, there emerges an

[29]   "The Symbolism of Poetry", *Essays*, 191-192.

image. Yet Yeats's "symbol" is not inherent in the object; it is evoked by the Great Mind which flows through all the objects in nature. The object itself is a medium, the poet an interpreter. The reader of Yeats's "symbol", therefore, will always discover part of the Great Mind, after their mind is freed from the restrictions of daily life. Pound makes no such guarantee. To Pound, liberation itself is the merit of poetic experience; it is the end, not a means toward the end. To recognize such a thing as the Great Mind might mean a commitment to another form of a rigid system, from which the mind has just been freed. In other words, Pound emphasizes the liberating function, Yeats the representative function. The freshness, the individuality, of the image becomes very important to Pound; a traditional image would shock no one, liberate no one; hence the importance of a personal image and the ineffectiveness of a historical image. But to Yeats it matters little whether the symbol is personal or traditional; importance lies in its evocative power; the traditional symbol may even have an advantage over its rival in that it connects the reader's mind to the common heritage of his race. The difference between Pound's "image" and Yeats's "symbol" again amounts to the difference of philosophical belief between the two men: the one believed in the essential oneness of all men, while the other emphasized the difference of one man or one experience from another.

Neither Zeami nor Bashō discusses the use of image, metaphor or symbol in poetry. It is not that the Japanese writers thought lightly of these literary devices; on the contrary these devices were so abundantly used in every work of their times that it had become a matter of course to employ them in writing. Japanese poets, to a far greater extent than Western poets in general, think and feel in terms of imagery; their poetry is full of visual and auditory images. The metaphorical pattern of thinking was primarily what attracted Yeats and Pound to Japanese literature. All poets, favoring intuition over logic, instinctively turn to metaphorical or symbolical writing. Zeami pursued this line to its end: in expounding his aesthetics, where a Western writer would have used a form of logical argumentation, he goes on with his metaphorical writing, comparing an aesthetic mood to a plant or describing a *nō* performance in terms of snow heaped in a silver bowl. Throughout Zeami's writings there lies, as we feel, a belief that an aesthetic effect cannot be logically analyzed or objectively documented, that it can only be presented by a metaphor, by some natural object which would produce a similar artistic effect in the participant's mind. It is images and symbols that produce aesthetic impact; logic brings only proof and argument. Thus the *nō* drama, aiming at the creation of certain moods, is full of passages united not so much by logic as by a mood. In some of the best *nō* plays the technique of the "Unifying Image" is used in order to achieve atmospheric coherence. In an emotionally heightened scene even grammatical coherence is broken, resulting in fragmentary phrases and clauses such as we often find in Symbolist or Surrealist poems. Pound, if he had been more familiar with the *nō* in the original Japanese, would have said that such uncompleted sentences are really closer to nature because no complete sentence exists in nature. But, besides producing a mood, images in the *nō* drama have another important function: they invoke a supernatural power. A good example is seen in the second act of the apparitional *nō*, where the monk puts forth the image of a lotus flower and prays the tormented sinner's soul into its rest. But in reality the whole *nō* drama is a symbolic ritual in which the "other world" is invoked through the incantation of the performers. As we saw in our first chapter, the monk is not only the redeemer of the sinner but the medium and symbol-maker who visualizes heaven and hell for us. Zeami's concept of the symbol here approaches Yeats's: the image or symbol is a manifestation of some superhuman power, something through which we glimpse the strange "other world".

Bashō does not seem to recognize such magical power in the image. To him a natural object is important, not because it represents certain superhuman power, but because it is an object, because it is part of nature. In this sense the image in

Bashō is not a metaphor nor a symbol; it does not stand for something else. What it presents is a vague feeling of nature, "impersonal mood", which is inherent in the image itself. The image in *haiku*, therefore, does not lead the reader to any super-human world; if it does, it takes us to the "unhuman" world. But this "unhuman" world is not a world at all, since it means a liberation from social and moral bonds; it is not confinement but freedom. At this point Bashō's idea of the image seems to move toward Pound's. Yet Bashō significantly differs from Pound in that this liberation is done in tranquillity, not in violence. The *haiku* poet brings together disparate images in such a way that they do not clash but blend in the same color (or colorlessness) of the "impersonal mood". This is foreign to Pound's method. If the unifying of images could be compared to the blending of water, Bashō's method is to quietly let fall a drop of pure water into a calm sea, and Pound's, at least in his mature years, is to pour pails of water, natural and artificial, into an ocean and stir it round into a whirlpool.

One interesting question in connection with the image is whether Zeami and Bashō took advantage of the pictorial nature of the Chinese characters they used. Since Chinese characters are ideographs, Japanese poets with an imagistic tendency may be tempted to use them quite profitably. The fact, however, is that neither Zeami nor Bashō made any attempt in that direction; nor, for that matter, did any other Japanese poet. The reason for this is rather simple. A Chinese character, when it is actually used in a word or phrase, is not taken by a Japanese (or Chinese) reader for an abbreviated picture or unit of pictures. It has lost its pictorial value. In the first place, there are only a small number of ideographs (all simple ones) whose meaning can be traced back to their origin in terms of imagery; the majority of Chinese characters are made up in such complex, irrational and ambiguous ways that etymologists themselves have great difficulty in analyzing them. In the second place, even with a simple character the reader does not recognize it as an image; he sees it as a unit of meaning, abstract or concrete. The reader, as soon as he sees the ideograph, grasps its meaning without analyzing it into its pictorial components. Furthermore in actual Japanese an ideograph usually appears in combination with other ideographs or with Japanese characters; it is not considered as an isolated unit, as in Pound's *Cantos*. For these reasons the ideographic value of Chinese characters has never been utilized in Japanese poetry. In fact, the earliest anthology of Japanese poetry used Chinese characters for their sound value in the main. The succeeding *waka* poets tried to get away from Chinese ideograms: they wrote their poems all in Japanese characters (which are phonetic symbols). They did think of the visual effect of their work, and they soon developed the art of calligraphy. If the poet wants to express his emotion in visual art as well as verbal, calligraphy is certainly a far more flexible, subtle and complex means of attaining his wish than printed ideograph. In *haiku*, therefore, calligraphy is often an important element; the *haiku* poet, when he writes down his poem, tries to express his feeling in his calligraphy as well. Bashō and some other *haiku* poets added painting to it, but they never talked of ideograph. Of course these arguments do not invalidate Pound's theory of ideograph, which, as we have already seen, is really a variation of metaphorical technique.

There remains just one more topic to be discussed: the function of literature. In the European tradition poetry has been considered *dulce* or *utile* – "pleasurable" or "useful" – and some writers and theorists have strongly emphasized only one of the pair. In English literature neo-classical authors stressed the didactic value of poetry; in Japanese literature the novelists of the late Tokugawa period carried the principle so far that didacticism frequently infringed upon the artistic merit of their work. On the other hand there have been conscious and unconscious practitioners of art for art's sake both in English and Japanese literature: the *fin de siècle* writers in English and some medieval court poets in Japanese. Yet it is clear that a great work of art does not rely on its didactic or hedonistic value alone, that it combines both. The pleasure which a work of art gives is a particular kind of pleasure which comes from its revelatory nature. The teaching which it contains is not a textbook lesson or religious preaching, but a non-acquisitive contemplation, a pleasurable seriousness. Evidently what is important is to determine the nature of aesthetic pleasure and aesthetic revelation which, both combined, constitute the function of poetry.

Zeami, as we have seen, stresses the hedonistic principle more than the didactic, since his immediate concern is a creation of beauty. The pleasure of art, in Zeami's view, comes from the spectacle of sheer beauty of form, movement and music: the pleasure one would get upon watching "a white bird with a flower in its beak". Young Yeats and young Pound had a similar view, as we have seen earlier in this chapter. Yet as they grew older they came to note the inadequacy of the Pre-Raphaelite view. Thus Yeats held that the pleasure of great art lay in "pure, aimless joy", but that the joy came from the mingling of contraries, from the fact that the soul had been freed from social and moral restrictions. Thus Pound affirmed that the beauty of art lay in the glow arising from its exact perception, that all great works of art were revelatory. Thus Zeami made his *yugen* and "the sublime" imply a certain attitude toward life, Buddhistic in nature. For Bashō the pleasure of art consists in a liberation from the worldly involvements, an escape from the ego. In general, we may say then, the pleasure of poetry lies in its beauty, but this beauty is not merely of a sensuous kind: it is a beauty which is derived from an acquisition of new knowledge. And new knowledge is gained when the mind is liberated from its ordinary confinement and enters a realm where it pursues its own desire, its own perfection. Perception is the cause, ecstasy the result.

This is a very romantic view. But in passing we may note that Bashō also held a more practical view on the function of poetry. He classified the practitioners of versification into three groups and found merit in each group. The first group includes petty poets who would do everything to win a prize at a poetry contest; though they are misinterpreters of the "poetic spirit", they help contest-judges to feed their families and contest-sponsors to increase their funds. The second group consists of wealthy men who enjoy their leisurely hours in a poetry contest, neither boasting of a victory if they win, nor irritated with a defeat if they lose. Though they are doing nothing more than a boy's game, they entertain with wine and feast the poverty-stricken poets who participate in the game as contestants or judges. Poets who belong to the third group are fewer than ten in the whole nation; they "try to improve the mind and ease the heart, make no unnecessary argument on other people's virtue or vice, and thereby seek to become a person qualified to enter the true way".[30] The first and second groups are false poets, poet-pretenders; but they are enjoying themselves, without doing harm to others. The third group of poets know that the true pleasure of *haiku* lies in entering a certain realm inaccessible to an average man under ordinary circumstances.

Every didactic view of poetry, if it ever wishes to escape from moral or political dogmatism, must be based on the principle which Bashō attributes to his third group: poetry introduces its reader into a new realm of knowledge, into a refreshing and enriching experience which he cannot possibly acquire in his daily life. What, then, is this new knowledge or poetic experience? This is a question which must be answered by each individual man, since it depends largely on the way in which each person interprets human life. To Zeami, the aim of poetic experience was to know the universal law which rules over man and nature, over the past and future life as well as the present. To Bashō it was to enter a realm where all personal emotions evaporate and only the feeling of impersonal nature remains. To Yeats it was to touch the Great Mind into which all individual passions flow, at times clashing but finally forming an harmonious whole as beautiful as a perfect human body. To Pound it was to find a truth which,

[30]    Letter to Kyokusui, 1694. *BI*, 709.

even though it may not be the whole truth, is at least a truth which exactly fits the particular situation. One common factor among these four is the function of poetry as a liberation of man from the common, petty self which lives in this world, the self controlled by the ego. It is, in brief, the liberation of man from mortality.

Here literature approaches religion, since religion also attempts man's liberation from the perishable world and the perishable self. Both art and religion strive to determine man's place in the changing universe, thereby giving him the center of perspective around which he organizes his experience. Science and philosophy cannot do this, because they deal only with objective and rational parts of human mind, only with physical and analyzable parts of the universe. Art and religion treat the whole of man, all aspects of life as an integrated entity. Zeami and Bashō saw art primarily in this capacity. But art, after all, is not religion, as these Japanese writers had to realize near their death. In religion, death is the final glory of man, of the enlightened man, which opens for him the door toward his union with the eternal. Religion must suppress the desires of humanity, the vitality in man which keeps him living on. But humanity is the very foundation on which art stands. Art realizes man's dreams, man's desires, man's concept of how life ought to be. Some artists, like Zeami and Bashō, may see art as something which helps man to renounce his desires. But no artist can completely destroy his desires; if he does, he will no longer be an artist because he has destroyed his desire to create, too. The dilemma of Zeami and Bashō lay precisely in this: they wanted religion, but religion, in turn, wanted them to abandon their art. Religion imposes restrictions upon a free expansion of man's faculties, while art enriches his life by nourishing his impulses. The Western poets escaped from this dilemma by believing that the development of man's faculties was an advancement toward God. They believed in anthropomorphic and humanistic religion. This attitude, however, ultimately led to the self-destruction of religion. The belief that God's creation is rational, and that man is capable of knowing all its secrets, was the beginning of modern science. Mistrust of the irrational quickly weakened the power of religion. For many modern artists in the West, therefore, art and religion are not in opposition but in one camp against the common enemy of science. But, between art and religion, the former looks more promising because it is broader, more inclusive and flexible. Thus Matthew Arnold and I. A. Richards have predicted that poetry will in time take the place of religion in society. The chief ground for their argument was that modern men can no longer believe in myths and superstitions of which religion is made, and that poetry can assimilate into itself scientific or philosophical views also. Science and religion appeal only to parts of man; poetry, to the whole of man. It is doubtful, however, that Arnold's and Richards' prediction will ever come true. Religion may have superstitions, but it is mystery so much the more; man, being both rational and irrational, needs something absolute which will justify his irrationality. Poetry will never be a substitute for religion, or vice versa. Nevertheless there is little doubt about the validity of the view that poetry can freely contain and assimilate all facts of life to a greater extent than any other branch of human knowledge. Poetry, more than anything else, can present life in its complexity, in its inclusiveness. It can present truth, or an equivalent of truth, with all its modifications. It is closer and more immediate to life than science, philosophy or religion, because it is less generalized. Poetry deals with the same themes as psychology, sociology or theology, with less abstraction and with more particularization. Mathematics, ethics and political science may go through drastic changes as time changes and place differs. But the basic concept of poetry has never changed and is unlikely to change as time or place changes, because poetry represents a more vital part of human life which transcends the temporal. It presents life in the way life is lived, internal or external, empirical or imaginative. And that is the main function of poetry.

# SELECTED BIBLIOGRAPHY

## I. IN ENGLISH

Alder, F. W., *Ezra Pound and the Art of Poetry* (University of Washington Master's Thesis). (Seattle, 1958).

Caldwell, James R., *John Keats' Fancy* (Ithaca, N.Y., 1945).

Coffman, Stanley K., *Imagism: A Chapter for the History of Modern Poetry* (Norman, 1951).

Eliot, T. S., *Selected Essays 1917-1932* (New York, 1932).

Ellmann, Richard, *The Identity of Yeats* (London, 1954).

——, *Yeats: The Man and the Masks* (New York, 1948).

Espey, John J., *Ezra Pound's Mauberley* (Berkeley, Calif., 1955).

Fenollosa, Ernest & Ezra Pound, *Certain Noble Plays of Japan* (Churchtown, 1916).

——, *"Noh", or Accomplishment* (London, 1916).

Gwynn, Stephen L., ed., *Scattering Branches: Tributes to the Memory of W. B. Yeats* (New York, 1940).

Hall, James & Martin Steinmann, eds., *The Permanence of Yeats* (New York, 1950).

Hausermann, H. W., "W. B. Yeats' Criticism of Ezra Pound", *English Studies*, XXIX (1948), 97-109.

Henn, Thomas R., *The Lonely Tower: Studies in the Poetry of W. B. Yeats* (London, 1950).

Hone, Joseph, *W. B. Yeats: 1865-1939* (New York, 1943).

Hughes, Glenn A., *Imagism and the Imagists* (Stanford, 1931).

Jeffares, A. N., *W. B. Yeats: Man and Poet* (London, 1949).

Keene, Donald, ed., *Anthology of Japanese Literature* (New York, 1955).

Keene, Donald, *Japanese Literature: An Introduction for Western Readers* (New York, 1955).

Kenner, Hugh, *The Poetry of Ezra Pound* (Norfolk, 1951).

Kermode, Frank, *Romantic Image* (London, 1957).

Konishi, Jin'ichi, "New Approaches to the Study of the Nō Drama", *Tokyō Kyōiku Daigaku Bungaku-bu Kiyō*, March, 1960.

McKinnon, Richard N., "The Nō and Zeami", *Far Eastern Quarterly*, XI (1952), 355-361.

——, "Zeami on the Art of Training", *Harvard Journal of Asiatic Studies*, XVI (1953), 200-225.

MacNiece, Louis, *The Poetry of W. B. Yeats* (London, 1941).

Menon, V. K. Narayana, *The Development of William Butler Yeats* (Edinburgh, 1942).

Miner, Earl, "Pound, *Haiku* and the Image", *Hudson Review*, IX (1956-57), 570-584.

———, *The Japanese Tradition in British and American Literature* (Princeton, 1958).

Miyamori, Asatarō, *An Anthology of Haiku, Ancient and Modern* (Tokyo, 1932).

Moore, Virginia, *The Unicorn: William Butler Yeats' Search for Reality* (New York, 1954).

Murasaki Shikibu, *A Wreath of Cloud* (the Third Part of *The Tale of Genji*), tr. Arthur Waley (Boston, 1927).

Pound, Ezra, *The ABC of Reading* (London, 1934).

———, *Antheil and the Treatise on Harmony* (Paris, 1924).

———, *The Cantos of Ezra Pound* (New York, 1948).

———, *Culture*, (Norfolk, 1938).

———, *Gaudier Brzeska* (London & New York, 1916).

———, *Guide to Kulchur* (Norfolk, 1952).

———, *Homage to Sextus Propertius* (London, 1934).

———, *How to Read* (Le Beausset, France, 1932).

———, *Hugh Selwyn Mauberley* (London, 1920).

———, *Impact: Essays on Ignorance and the Decline of American Civilization*, ed., Noel Stock (Chicago, 1960).

———, *Instigations* (New York, 1920).

———, *The Letters of Ezra Pound*, ed., D. D. Paige (New York, 1950).

———, *Literary Essays of Ezra Pound*, ed., T. S. Eliot (Norfolk, 1954).

———, *Make It New* (New Haven, 1935).

———, *Patria Mia* (Chicago, 1950).

———, *Pavannes and Divigations* (Norfolk, 1958).

———, *Pavannes and Divisions* (New York, 1918).

———, *Personae* (New York, 1926).

———, *Polite Essays* (Norfolk, n. d.).

———, *The Spirit of Romance* (Norfolk, 1952).

———, *The Translations of Ezra Pound* (Norfolk, 1950).

Ramsey, Warren, *Jules Laforgue and the Ironic Inheritance* (New York, 1953).

Richards, I. A., *Principles of Literary Criticism* (London, 1924).

Russell, Peter, ed., *An Examination of Ezra Pound* (Norfolk, 1950).

Smith, J. H. & E. W. Parks, eds., *The Great Critics: An Anthology of Literary Criticism* (New York, 1951).

Stallman, R. W., ed., *The Critic's Notebook* (Minneapolis, 1950).

Stauffer, Donald A., *The Golden Nightingale: Essays on Some Principles of Poetry in the Lyrics of W. B. Yeats* (New York, 1949).

Toki, Zemmaro, *Japanese Nō Plays* (Tokyo, 1954).

Tsunoda, Ryusaku, William Theodore de Bary, & Donald Keene, eds., *Sources of Japanese Tradition* (New York, 1958).

Unterecker, John E., *A Reader's Guide to William Butler Yeats* (New York, 1959).

Wade, Allan, *A Bibliography of the Writings of W. B. Yeats* (London, 1951).

Waley, Arthur, *The Nō Plays of Japan* (New York, 1922).

Wellek, René & Austin Warren, *Theory of Literature*, 2nd ed. (New York, 1956).

Wilson, F. A. C. C., *W. B. Yeats and Tradition* (London, 1958).

Wimsatt, William K., Jr. & Cleanth Brooks, *Literary Criticism: A Short History* (New York, 1957).

Winters, Yvor, *In Defense of Reason* (Denver, 1947).

West, Ray B., ed., *Essays in Modern Literary Criticism* (New York, 1952).

Yeats, William Butler, *Autobiography* (New York, 1953).

——, *The Collected Poems of W. B. Yeats*, definitive edition (New York, 1957).

——, *The Collected Works of William Butler Yeats*. 8 vols. (London, 1908).

——, *The Cutting of an Agate* (New York, 1912).

——, *Essays* (New York, 1924).

——, *Essays, 1931 to 1936* (Dublin, 1937).

——, *Four Plays for Dancers* (New York, 1921).

——, *If I were Four-and-Twenty* (Dublin, 1940).

——, *The Letters of W. B. Yeats*, ed., Allan Wade (New York, 1955).

——, *Letters on Poetry from W. B. Yeats to Dorothy Wellesley*, ed. Dorothy Wellesley (London & New York, 1940).

——, *Letters to Katharine Tynan*, ed., Roger McHugh (New York, 1953).

——, *On the Boiler* (Dublin, 1938).

——, ed., *The Oxford Book of Modern Verse: 1892-1935* (New York, 1937).

——, *Pages from a Diary Written in Nineteen Hundred and Thirty* (Dublin, 1944).

——, *Plays and Controversies* (London, 1923).

——, "Poetry and Patriotism", W. B. Yeats & Lionel Johnson, *Poetry and Ireland* (Churchtown, 1908), 1-18.

——, *A Vision* (London, 1925).

——, *A Vision: A Reissue with the Author's Final Revisions* (New York, 1956).

——, *Wheels and Butterflies* (New York, 1935).

Zabel, M. D., ed., *Literary Opinion in America* (New York, 1951).

## II. IN JAPANESE

安倍能成「能樂雜叢」東京, 1948.

有島生馬「能の繪畫美」能樂全書 第6卷, 59-81.

荒木良雄「中世文學の形成と發展」東京, 1957.

穎原退藏他「芭蕉講座」改訂四版, 東京, 1956.

穎原退藏「芭蕉去來」大阪, 1941.

————「"輕み"の眞義」芭蕉研究 II (1943), 32-34.

————校訂「去來抄・三册子・旅寢論」東京, 1939.

藤井和義「中世文學の主體的精神」東京, 1944.

廣末保「元祿文學研究」東京, 1957.

久松潛一「日本文學評論史」古代中世篇・形態論篇・
    東京, 1936,47.

池田廣司. 小林責「能狂言研究史」國文學解釋と鑑賞.
    XXIII (1958), no. 10. 195–224.

井本農一,栗山理一,中村俊定編「芭蕉」國語國文學研
—   究史大成 12. 東京. 1959.

井本農一「俳文芸の論」東京. 1953.

神田豐穗編「芭蕉一代集」日本俳書大系・芭蕉時代1
    東京. 1926.

————「蕉門俳諧前集」同上・芭蕉時代 2.

————「蕉門俳諧後集」同上・芭蕉時代 3.

————「蕉門俳話文集」同上・芭蕉時代 4.

觀世壽夫「現代の能に於ける傳統の問題」文學. XXV
    (1957), 1045–50.

唐木順三「中世の文學」東京. 1955.

————「能の魅力」文學 XXV (1957), 1067–1072.

川瀬一馬「頭註世阿彌二十三部集」東京. 1945.

小林靜雄「世阿彌」東京. 1943.

小林智昭「世阿彌研究—心の論理」國語と國文學
    XXIX (1952), no.5. 17–27.

小宮豐隆「芭蕉の研究」東京. 1933.

————「能と歌舞伎」東京. 1935.

————「能と狂言」國文學解釋と鑑賞 XXII (1958), no.
    10. 2–6.

栗山理一「俳味」國文學解釋と鑑賞 XXV (1960), no.5. 8–13.

桑田忠親「世阿彌と利休」東京. 1956.

中島斌雄「芭蕉の風雅」國文學解釋と鑑賞 XIV (1949),
    no. 11. 28–34.

中村草田男「体験の季題」國文學解釋と鑑賞 XXV (1960),
    no. 5. 21–26.

新關良三「日本演劇論」東京. 1942.

西尾實「中世詩としての蕉風俳諧」文學. XVIII (1950),
    393–402.

————「歌舞劇としての能」國文學解釋と鑑賞 XXIII
    (1958), no. 10. 7–10.

西下經一,栗山理一「日本文學の美的理念」國文學解
    釋と鑑賞 XXIII (1958), no. 12. 38–94.

野上豐一郎編「能樂全書」6卷. 東京. 1942-44.

野上豐一郎「能. 研究と發見」東京. 1930.

能勢朝次「芭蕉の俳諧精神」芭蕉研究 II (1943), 16-31.

――――「芭蕉の俳論」京都. 1948.

――――「俳論研究の動向」國文學解釋と鑑賞 XIV (1949), no. 11. 22-28.

――――「能樂研究」東京. 1952.

――――「三册子評釋」東京. 1954.

――――「幽玄論」東京. 1944.

――――「世阿彌十六部集評釋」2卷. 東京. 1940,44.

能勢朝次・守隨憲治・小宮豐隆「能狂言淨瑠璃歌舞伎」東京. 1951.

岡崎義惠「芭蕉の芸術」東京. 1959.

――――「芭蕉を中心としたる俳諧の氣分内容」國語と國文學 I (1924). 840-877.

――――「文芸學からみた日本美」國文學解釋と鑑賞 XXIII (1958), no. 12. 2-9.

――――「芸術論の探求」東京. 1941.

――――「俳諧と連歌」國文學解釋と鑑賞 XXV (1960), no. 5. 2-8.

――――「謠曲における象徵」文學 XI (1943), 183-196.

表章「世阿彌から禪竹へ」國文學解釋と鑑賞 XXIII (1958) no. 10. 57-63.

佐成謙太郎「謠曲大觀」7卷東京 1929-30.

佐々木信綱編「日本歌學大系」第3卷. 東京. 1941.

志田義秀「芭蕉と制作意識」芭蕉研究 I (1942), 14-25.

杉浦正一郎「芭蕉研究」東京. 1958.

――――「芭蕉集」現代語譯日本古典文學全集. 東京. 1956.

高橋義孝「能の美學的考察」文學. XXV (1957). 1028-35.

高村光太郎「能の彫刻美」能樂全書. 第6卷. 83-89.

土岐善麿「文學としての能の脚本」國文學解釋と鑑賞. 69-74.

臼井吉見「芭蕉に於ける虛構の意味」文學. XX (1952). 117-124.

山崎喜好「細道の旅と俳論」芭蕉研究 III (1947). 46-70.

横道万里雄「能の戲曲論的考察」文學. XXI (1953). 377-384.

# INDEX